Practical Cassandra

The Addison-Wesley Data and Analytics Series

Visit informit.com/awdataseries for a complete list of available publications.

The Addison-Wesley Data and Analytics Series provides readers with practical knowledge for solving problems and answering questions with data. Titles in this series primarily focus on three areas:

1. **Infrastructure:** how to store, move, and manage data
2. **Algorithms:** how to mine intelligence or make predictions based on data
3. **Visualizations:** how to represent data and insights in a meaningful and compelling way

The series aims to tie all three of these areas together to help the reader build end-to-end systems for fighting spam; making recommendations; building personalization; detecting trends, patterns, or problems; and gaining insight from the data exhaust of systems and user interactions.

Make sure to connect with us!
informit.com/socialconnect

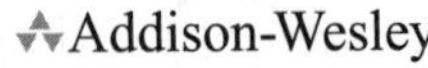

Safari Books Online

ALWAYS LEARNING PEARSON

Practical Cassandra

A Developer's Approach

Russell Bradberry
Eric Lubow

Addison-Wesley

Upper Saddle River, NJ • Boston • Indianapolis • San Francisco
New York • Toronto • Montreal • London • Munich • Paris • Madrid
Capetown • Sydney • Tokyo • Singapore • Mexico City

For information about buying this title in bulk quantities, or for special sales opportunities (which may include electronic versions; custom cover designs; and content particular to your business, training goals, marketing focus, or branding interests), please contact our corporate sales department at corpsales@pearsoned.com or (800) 382-3419.

For government sales inquiries, please contact governmentsales@pearsoned.com.

For questions about sales outside the U.S., please contact international@pearsoned.com.

Visit us on the Web: informit.com/aw

Cataloging-in-Publication Data is on file with the Library of Congress.

ISBN-13: 978-0-321-93394-2
ISBN-10: 0-321-93394-X

Text printed in the United States on recycled paper at RR Donnelley in Crawfordsville, Indiana.
First printing, December 2013

❖

This book is for the community. We have been a part of the Cassandra community for a few years now, and they have been fantastic every step of the way. This book is our way of giving back to the people who have helped us and have allowed us to help pave the way for the future of Cassandra.

❖

Contents

Foreword by Jonathon Ellis

I was excited to learn that *Practical Cassandra* would be released right at my five-year anniversary of working on Cassandra. During that time, Cassandra has achieved its goal of offering the world's most reliable and performant scalable database. Along the way, Cassandra has changed significantly, and a modern book is, at this point, overdue. Eric and Russell were early adopters of Cassandra at SimpleReach; in *Practical Cassandra*, you benefit from their experience in the trenches administering Cassandra, developing against it, and building one of the first CQL drivers.

If you are deploying Cassandra soon, or you inherited a Cassandra cluster to tend, spend some time with the deployment, performance tuning, and maintenance chapters. Some complexity is inherent in a distributed system, particularly one designed to push performance limits and scale without compromise; forewarned is, as they say, forearmed. If you are new to Cassandra, I highly recommend the chapters on data modeling and CQL. The Cassandra Query Language represents a major shift in developing against Cassandra and dramatically lowers the learning curve from what you may expect or fear.

Here's to the next five years of progress!

—Jonathon Ellis, Apache Cassandra Chair

Foreword by Paul Dix

Cassandra is quickly becoming one of the backbone components for anyone working with large datasets and real-time analytics. Its ability to scale horizontally to handle hundreds of thousands (or millions) of writes per second makes it a great choice for high-volume systems that must also be highly available. That's why I'm very pleased that this book is the first in the series to cover a key infrastructural component for the Addison-Wesley Data & Analytics Series: the data storage layer.

In 2011, I was making my second foray into working with Cassandra to create a high-volume, scalable time series data store. At the time, Cassandra 0.8 had been released, and the path to 1.0 was fairly clear, but the available literature was lagging sorely behind. This book is exactly what I could have used at the time. It provides a great introduction to setting up and modeling your data in Cassandra. It has coverage of the most recent features, including CQL, sets, maps, and lists. However, it doesn't stop with the introductory stuff. There's great material on how to run a cluster in production, how to tune performance, and on general operational concerns.

I can't think of more qualified users of Cassandra to bring this material to you. Eric and Russell are Datastax Cassandra MVPs and have been working extensively with Cassandra and running it in production for years. Thankfully, they've done a great job of distilling their experience into this book so you won't have to search for insight into how to develop against and run the most current release of Cassandra.

—Paul Dix, Series Editor

Preface

Apache Cassandra is a massively scalable, open-source, NoSQL database. Cassandra is best suited to applications that need to store large amounts of structured, semistructured, and unstructured data. Cassandra offers asynchronous masterless replication to nodes in many data centers. This gives it the capability to have no single point of failure while still offering low latency operations.

When we first embarked on the journey of writing a book, we had one goal in mind: We wanted to keep the book easily digestible by someone just getting started with Cassandra, but also make it a useful reference guide for day-to-day maintenance, tuning, and troubleshooting. We know the pain of scouring the Internet only to find outdated and contrived examples of how to get started with a new technology. We hope that *Practical Cassandra* will be the go-to guide for developers—both new and at an intermediate level—to get up and running with as little friction as possible.

This book describes, in detail, how to go from nothing to a fully functional Cassandra cluster. It shows how to bring up a cluster of Cassandra servers, choose the appropriate configuration options for the cluster, model your data, and monitor and troubleshoot any issues. Toward the end of the book, we provide sample code, in-depth detail as to how Cassandra works under the covers, and real-world case studies from prominent users.

What's in This Book?

This book is intended to guide a developer in getting started with Cassandra, from installation to common maintenance tasks to writing an application. If you are just starting with Cassandra, this book will be most helpful when read from start to finish. If you are familiar with Cassandra, you can skip around the chapters to easily find what you need.

- Chapter 1, Introduction to Cassandra: This chapter gives an introduction to Cassandra and the philosophies and history of the project. It provides an overview of terminology, what Cassandra is best suited for, and, most important what we hope to accomplish with this book.
- Chapter 2, Installation: Chapter 2 is the start-to-finish guide to getting Cassandra up and running. Whether the installation is on a single node or a large cluster, this chapter guides you through the process. In addition to cluster setup, the most important configuration options are outlined.
- Chapter 3, Data Modeling: Data modeling is one of the most important aspects of using Cassandra. Chapter 3 discusses the primary differences between Cassandra

and traditional RDBMSs, as well as going in depth into different design patterns, philosophies, and special features that make Cassandra the data store of tomorrow.

- Chapter 4, CQL: CQL is Cassandra's answer to SQL. While not a full implementation of SQL, CQL helps to bridge the gap when transitioning from an RDBMS. This chapter explores in depth the features of CQL and provides several real-world examples of how to use it.
- Chapter 5, Deployment and Provisioning: After you've gotten an overview of installation and querying, this chapter guides you through real-world deployment and resource provisioning. Whether you plan on deploying to the cloud or on bare-metal hardware, this chapter is for you. In addition to outlining provisioning in various types of configurations, it discusses the impact of the different configuration options and what is best for different types of workloads.
- Chapter 6, Performance Tuning: Now that you have a live production cluster deployed, this chapter guides you through tweaking the Cassandra dials to get the most out of your hardware, operating system, and the Java Virtual Machine (JVM).
- Chapter 7, Maintenance: Just as with everything in life, the key to having a performant and, more important, working Cassandra cluster is to maintain it properly. Chapter 7 describes all the different tools that take the headache out of maintaining the components of your system.
- Chapter 8, Monitoring: Any systems administrator will tell you that a healthy system is a monitored system. Chapter 8 outlines the different types of monitoring options, tools, and what to look out for when administering a Cassandra cluster.
- Chapter 9, Drivers and Sample Code: Now that you have a firm grasp on how to manage and maintain your Cassandra cluster, it is time to get your feet wet. In Chapter 9, we discuss the different drivers and driver features offered in various languages. We then go for the deep dive by presenting a working example application in not only one, but four of the most commonly used languages: Java, C#, Ruby, and Python.
- Chapter 10, Troubleshooting: Now that you have written your sample application, what happens when something doesn't quite work right? Chapter 10 outlines the tools and techniques that can be used to get your application back on the fast track.
- Chapter 11, Architecture: Ever wonder what goes on under the Cassandra "hood"? In this chapter, we discuss how Cassandra works, how it keeps your data safe and accurate, and how it achieves such blazingly fast performance.
- Chapter 12, Case Studies: So who uses Cassandra, and how? Chapter 12 presents three case studies from forward-thinking companies that use Cassandra in unique ways. You will get the perspective straight from the mouths of the developers at Ooyala, Hailo, and eBay.

- Appendix A, Getting Help: Whether you're stuck on a confusing problem or just have a theoretical question, having a place to go for help is paramount. This appendix tells you about the best places to get that help.
- Appendix B, Enterprise Cassandra: There are many reasons to use Cassandra, but sometimes it may be better for you to focus on your organization's core competencies. This appendix describes a few companies that can help you leverage Cassandra efficiently and effectively while letting you focus on what you do best.

Code Samples

All code samples and more in-depth examples can be found on GitHub at http://devdazed.github.io/practical-cassandra/.

Acknowledgments

We would like to acknowledge everyone involved with Cassandra and the Cassandra community—everyone from the core contributors of Cassandra all the way down to the end users who have made it such a popular platform to work with. Without the community, Cassandra wouldn't be where it is today. Special thanks go to

- Jay Patel for putting together the eBay case study
- Al Tobey and Evan Chan for putting together the case study on Ooyala
- Dominic Wong for putting together the Hailo case study
- All the technical reviewers, including Adam Chalemian, Mark Herschberg, Joe Stein, and Bryan Smith, who helped give excellent feedback and ensured technical accuracy where possible
- Paul Dix for setting us up and getting us on the right track with writing

About the Authors

Russell Bradberry (Twitter: @devdazed) is the principal architect at SimpleReach, where he is responsible for designing and building out highly scalable, high-volume, distributed data solutions. He has brought to market a wide range of products, including a real-time bidding ad server, a rich media ad management tool, a content recommendation system, and, most recently, a real-time social intelligence platform. He is a U.S. Navy veteran, a DataStax MVP for Apache Cassandra, and the author of the NodeJS Cassandra driver Helenus.

Eric Lubow (Twitter: @elubow) is currently chief technology officer of SimpleReach, where he builds highly scalable, distributed systems for processing social data. He began his career building secure Linux systems. Since then he has worked on building and administering various types of ad systems, maintaining and deploying large-scale Web applications, and building email delivery and analytics systems. He is also a U.S. Army combat veteran and a DataStax MVP for Apache Cassandra.

Eric and Russ are regular speakers about Cassandra and distributed systems, and both live in New York City.

1

Introduction to Cassandra

Apache Cassandra is a powerful and massively scalable NoSQL database. It is architected to handle real-time big-data workloads across multiple data centers with no single point of failure. It works on commodity hardware and can easily be deployed in a cloud-based infrastructure. But before we get into the nitty-gritty of things, here is a quick lesson in Greek mythology.

A Greek Story

In Greek mythology, Cassandra was the beautiful daughter of King Priam and Queen Hecuba of Troy, the twin sister of Helenus and younger sister to the great Trojan warrior Hector, and eventually a priestess of Apollo. She was believed to be the second-most beautiful woman in the world. Her beauty was compared to the likes of Aphrodite or Helen of Troy. She had red curly hair, blue eyes, and fair skin and was intelligent, charming, friendly, and very desirable. The other side of Cassandra was that she was generally considered to be insane.

When Apollo first saw Cassandra, he immediately fell in love with her. To show his love, he offered her the gift of prophecy if she would kiss him, and she agreed. But when Apollo went to kiss Cassandra, instead of a kiss, she spat in his mouth. Because Apollo had already granted Cassandra the gift of prophecy, he could not take it away. But he did change it so that even though Cassandra would always know what was going to happen, nobody would ever believe her.

And in fabled fashion, when Cassandra told the people of Troy that the Trojan Horse was bad news, they ignored her and Troy was captured. After the Trojans lost the war, a Greek warrior named Ajax took Cassandra prisoner and gave her to King Agamemnon as a slave. She told Agamemnon that his wife, Clytemnestra, was going to kill him. But Apollo's curse did not allow anyone to believe her. After killing her husband, King Agamemnon, Clytemnestra then killed Cassandra.

The reason for telling this story is twofold. First, it shows a little about why the name Cassandra was chosen for this database. She was a repository of knowledge of things that were going to happen. This is similar to the way you can use the Cassandra system to help you build a better product by having a keen understanding of what's going on around you.

Second, the names of many of the characters in this and other Greek tragedies are used for the names of many of the applications that play well with Cassandra. These include Helenus (the Node.js driver), Priam (a Cassandra automation tool), and Hector (the Java driver), just to name a few.

What Is NoSQL?

There is no single definition for NoSQL. To some it stands for "Not Only SQL"; to others it means "No SQL." Either way, it refers to the departure from the traditional relational database technologies that have dominated the development landscape for the past few decades.

What is likely the largest driver of the NoSQL movement is a commonly held belief that relational databases are not well suited to large amounts of data and scale. Whether or not this is true, the emergence of the key/value, graph, document, and "big table" data storage engines shows that a new generation of database technologies is taking center stage.

There is no single database technology that is synonymous with the NoSQL movement. Branding and marketing seem to be mostly what determine how relevant a technology is to the terminology.

There's No Such Thing as "Web Scale"

Another marketing term that gets thrown around quite frequently is "Web scale." It is used quite often when discussing how to determine whether a database system is suitable for a particular Web application's needs and whether it will hold up as the application grows. This is a very subjective term as everyone's needs are different. A simple SQL setup will achieve most scalability needs. Depending on the read/write patterns of an application, one may need a specialized database, such as Kyoto Cabinet (previously named Tokyo Cabinet) for key/value or MongoDB as a document store. In a system that needs high write throughput and linear scalability, Cassandra is a great fit and will hold up under some very heavy workloads.

The key point to remember when discussing the idea of Web scale technologies is that nearly everything out there will scale with enough money, hardware, and headaches. The trick is to figure out which piece of software is best suited for your usage patterns and workloads and will scale out in a way suitable for your application and your organization.

ACID, CAP, and BASE

Before we get too deep into Cassandra, it is important to understand some of the basic concepts that surround databases so you know what concessions you may have to make when choosing a system. There are three main sets of properties that define what database systems are capable of. Those are ACID, CAP, and BASE. ACID comprises some of the general properties of database systems. CAP covers a little more about distributed systems. BASE is a little newer theory and includes the practical considerations of implementing a distributed system.

Understanding these theories will help you to understand where some of the design decisions come in, not only for Cassandra but also for your application and how it is developed. The idea of building distributed applications and distributed systems often comes down to give and take. You may give up consistency for availability. You may find it's wiser for your application's needs to give a little on availability in favor of consistency. ACID, CAP, and BASE are the driving technical theories behind many of these decisions. It is important to understand the trade-offs made in the design of the underlying systems (Cassandra) so you can ensure that your application performs the way you expect it to perform.

ACID

ACID stands for **A**tomicity, **C**onsistency, **I**solation, and **D**urability. In order to understand ACID and how it relates to databases, we need to talk about transactions. When it comes to databases, a transaction is defined as a single logical operation. For example, if you are shopping online, every time you add an item to your shopping cart, that item and its quantity make up the database transaction. Even if you add multiple items or multiple quantities of the same item with a single click, that entire shopping cart addition is just a single transaction.

Atomicity means that each transaction either works or it doesn't. This is to say that if any single part of the transaction fails, the entire transaction fails. This should hold true for every situation related to a transaction that could cause a failure. Network failure, power outage, or even a node outage occurring at transaction time should cause a complete transaction failure in an atomic system.

Consistency ensures that when a transaction is complete, whether it is successful or not, the database is still in a valid state. This means that any data written to the database must also be valid. When writing data to the database, you also need to include any database application-level rules such as constraints, cascades, triggers, or stored procedures. The application of those rules should also leave the data in a valid state.

Isolation is a property that ensures that all transactions that are run concurrently appear as if they were executed serially (one right after the other). Each transaction must be run in a vacuum (isolation). This is to say that if two transactions are run at the same time, they remain independent of each other during the transaction. Some examples of isolation are locks (table, row, column, etc.), dirty reads, and deadlocks. The reason these are relevant is concurrency. Multiple changes can be attempted on the same data or set of data. Knowing what version of the data is the correct one is important for keeping the entire system in a sane state.

Durability means that after the transaction is complete, it will remain that way. In other words, the data change that is incurred by the transaction is stored permanently, regardless of external events (such as a power failure).

CAP

The CAP theorem, also known as Brewer's theorem, asserts that it is impossible for a distributed system to satisfy all three CAP guarantees. CAP stands for **C**onsistency,

Availability, and **P**artition tolerance. The important thing to note about the CAP theorem is that all three parts of it cannot be satisfied at the same time.

Although the *C* in CAP also stands for "consistency" (similar to the *C* in ACID), the meaning is different. *Consistency* means that all nodes in a grouping see the same data at the same time. In other words, any particular query hitting any node in the system will return the same result for that specific query. Consistency also further implies that when a query updates a value in one node, the data will be updated to reflect the new value prior to the next query.

The *availability* of a system speaks to the guarantee that regardless of the success or failure of a request, the requestor will receive a response. This means that system operations will be able to continue even if part of the system is down, whatever the reason. Availability is what lets the software attempt to cope with and compensate for externalities such as hardware failures, network outages, power failures, and the like.

Partition tolerance refers to the capability of a distributed system to effectively distribute the load across multiple nodes. The load could be data or queries. This implies that even if a few nodes are down, the system will continue to function. Sharding is a commonly used management technique for distributing load across a cluster. Sharding, which is similar to horizontal partitioning, is a way of splitting data into separate parts and moving them to another server or physical location, generally for performance improvements.

There are various reasons that all three parts of the theorem cannot be satisfied in distributed systems. Most have to do with the volume of the data and how long it takes to move data around and check to ensure that it is correct. CAP is often used to justify the use of weaker consistency models. Many of the CAP-based ideas have evolved into the idea of BASE.

BASE

Just as in chemistry, BASE is at the opposite end of the spectrum from ACID. BASE stands for **B**asically **A**vailable, **S**oft state, and **E**ventual consistency. The notion of BASE comes in when dealing with a distributed system so large that maintaining the principles of CAP becomes impractical. It is worth noting that the constraints on transactions from ACID are still in play at some level; they just happen at different times with slightly different rules.

Having a system be *basically available* means that the system will respond to any request. The caveat is that the response may be a failure to get the data or that the data may be in an inconsistent or changing state. This is equivalent in the real world to depositing a check in your bank account and waiting for it to go through the clearinghouse to make the funds available to you.

Using the BASE terminology, we can expand on the idea of banking with checks. If your bank has only one branch, consistency and availability are satisfied. No partitioning is necessary, and every transaction you make will be available and consistent with itself. If your bank has two branches, when you deposit a check into branch A, branch B will not see the funds instantaneously because the data needs time to become eventually consistent. What if you deposit two checks and one bounces? The entire transaction should not fail because of one check; each check will be processed in isolation. A problem with one check should not cause a problem with the whole system. That would not make for a very durable system. If the computers at branch A go down, that shouldn't stop branch B from working completely. That would mean that the system isn't very available, so there are safety nets in place.

The idea of a *soft-state* system means the system is always changing. This is typically due to eventual consistency. It is common for soft-state systems to undergo changes even when there is no additional input to them.

Eventual consistency refers to the concept that once a system stops receiving input, the data will propagate to wherever else it needs to be in the system sooner or later. The beauty of this is that the system does not check for consistency on every transaction as is expected in an ACID-compliant system.

Where Cassandra Fits In

Now that we have a decent idea of the tenets of a distributed system, it's time to take a look at where Cassandra excels. There are a lot of database systems, and nearly all of them were designed to handle a particular problem efficiently and effectively. But the most important thing that you need to know when deciding whether Cassandra is the right tool for the job is the goal of the job. In other words, if you can illustrate what it is you are trying to accomplish, you'll be able to determine if Cassandra is what you need to be successful.

In the context of the Web analytics application that we are building, Cassandra is suitable for a variety of reasons. One of the most common use cases for Cassandra is dealing with time-series data. What this means is that there is a sequence of successive data points that are all related to the same topic. For example, every time a page view happens on your Web site, an entry is made into the logs with the time of the event (page view), including some metadata around that event (IP, browser, URL, etc.).

Now let's say your Web site isn't made up of just one or two Web servers, but a whole cluster of Web servers is required to support your traffic. And let's also say that you want to store the resulting Web server data in a database and not just aggregate logs on a log server. How is Cassandra well suited for that? Before you can answer whether or not Cassandra is the right tool to help you solve your problem, we should talk about what Cassandra is and where it came from.

What Is Cassandra?

Cassandra is an open-source distributed database management system. It is designed to handle large amounts of data spread across many commodity servers while remaining highly available. Cassandra is loosely defined as a key/value store where one key can map to one or more values.

Although early in its life Cassandra was just a key/value store, it has evolved into much more. It is now commonly seen as a hybrid containing common properties of two types of databases: a key/value store and a row store. Unlike a relational database management system (RDBMS), Cassandra ColumnFamilys (similar to relational tables) do not need to have matching columns within a row. Even rows within a ColumnFamily are not required to always follow the same naming schema. The options are available, but data patterns are not strictly enforced. Data can also be added in very high volumes at very high velocities, and Cassandra will determine the correct version of a piece of data by resolving the timestamp at which it was inserted into the system.

Architecturally, its decentralized nature allows for no single point of failure and ensures that every node in the cluster has the same role. This means that every node in the cluster can serve any request. Cassandra also supports replication and multi-data-center replication. Since replication strategies are configurable, you can set up your distribution architecture to be as centralized or spread out, or as redundant or fail-safe, as you would like. Because data is automatically replicated to nodes, downed or faulty nodes are easily replaceable. New nodes can be added at will, without downtime, to increase read and write throughput or even just availability. The consistency levels are tunable, which allows you to have the application enforce the amount of resources applied to data assurance at a transaction level.

Cassandra also has an ecosystem being built around it. There are monitoring systems like OpsCenter to help you see the health of your cluster and manage common administration tasks. There are drivers for many of the major languages. Cassandra now comes with integration points for Hadoop and MapReduce support, full text search with Solr, and Apache Pig and Hive support. There is even a SQL-like query language called CQL, or Cassandra Query Language, to help in the data modeling and access patterns.

History of Cassandra

Apache Cassandra was originally developed at Facebook in 2008 to power Facebook's in-box search feature. The original authors were Avinash Lakshman, who also is one of the authors of the Amazon Dynamo paper, and Prashant Malik. After being in production at Facebook for a while, Cassandra was released as an open-source project on Google Code in July of 2008. In March of 2009, it was accepted to the Apache Foundation as an incubator project. In February of 2010, it became a top-level Apache project.

As of the time of this writing, the most recent version of Apache Cassandra is the 1.2 series. Cassandra has come a long way since the first major release after its graduation to a top-level Apache project. It has picked up support for Hadoop, text search integration through Solr, CQL, zero-downtime upgrades, virtual nodes (vnodes), and self-tuning caches, just to name a few of the major features. Cassandra is still in constant heavy development, and new features are always being added and tested.

> **Note**
>
> The central paper on Cassandra, written by the primary Facebook engineers, is called "Cassandra—A Decentralized Structured Storage System" and is available at www.cs.cornell.edu/projects/ladis2009/papers/lakshman-ladis2009.pdf.

Schema-less (If You Want)

Cassandra ColumnFamilys are considered schema-less. This means that you do not need to define a schema ahead of time. If you want to add a column, you simply specify the column name at write-time and the column will be created if it doesn't exist. This lends itself to allowing for extremely wide rows, even rows that have millions of columns. Additionally, rows do not need to contain all or even any of the columns that other rows in the same table contain.

Cassandra does give you the option to create a schema, however. If you know what your data structure looks like, you can add column names and specify default types for those columns. This also enables you to add secondary indexes for the columns that you know about.

Who Uses Cassandra?

Cassandra is in wide use around the world, and usage is growing all the time. Companies like Netflix, eBay, Twitter, Reddit, and Ooyala all use Cassandra to power pieces of their architecture, and it is critical to the day-to-day operations of those organizations. To date, the largest publicly known Cassandra cluster by machine count has over 300TB of data spanning 400 machines.

Because of Cassandra's ability to handle high-volume data, it works well for a myriad of applications. This means that it's well suited to handling projects from the high-speed world of advertising technology in real time to the high-volume world of big-data analytics and everything in between. It is important to know your use case before moving forward to ensure things like proper deployment and good schema design.

Is Cassandra Right for Me?

This isn't a very easy question to answer. Using Cassandra requires thinking in a different way about how you store data. While there are rows and columns, Cassandra is, at its base, a key/value store. There is no built-in full text search; there are no B-tree indexes or data manipulation functions.

One of the biggest differences between Cassandra and standard SQL RDBMSs is that there are no manipulation functions. These include `SUM`, `GROUP`, `JOIN`, `MAX`, `MIN`, and any other method you would use to modify the data at query time.

While deciding if Cassandra is a good fit for your use case, know that a lot of data manipulation can be achieved at write-time rather than read-time. This, of course, means that you will be storing different views of the same data in multiple places. This is not necessarily a bad thing.

One example of this is to use counter columns where you would need aggregation. This is as easy as incrementing a value for each of the different ways you want to see your data. This pattern does require that you know what questions you want to ask ahead of time; if you need ad hoc data analysis in real time, Cassandra may not be the right fit.

Cassandra Terminology

In order to understand Cassandra, a good place to start is the vocabulary.

Cluster

A cluster is two or more Cassandra instances working together. These instances communicate with each other using the Gossip protocol.

Homogeneous Environment

Cassandra is considered homogeneous. This means that each and every Cassandra node contains everything required to complete a cluster. This differs from other systems such as HBase, which have master servers, region servers, ZooKeeper servers, and other different types of nodes. With Cassandra, expanding a cluster is as easy as adding a new node that is identical to every other node with the exception of the configuration and data for which it is responsible. This takes some complexity out of managing an infrastructure with many nodes.

Node

A node is an instance of Cassandra. A Cassandra cluster is made up of many nodes. If you are building a test cluster on a single machine and have multiple instances of Cassandra running, each instance would be considered a node.

Replication Factor

Replication factor (RF) is a setting on a keyspace that determines how many copies of the data will reside in the cluster. A replication factor of 3 means that there will be three copies of the data within a cluster. The replication factor also determines the number of nodes that return when using quorum reads/writes. A quorum read/write means that the query will be sent to (RF/2 + 1). Given an RF of 3, the query will be sent to two nodes (decimals are always rounded down). If you always do quorum reads and writes, you will always have consistent responses as at least one node in the replica set has the data that is being queried.

Tunable Consistency

Because different reads/writes may have different needs in terms of consistency, you can specify the consistency at read/write-time. Consistency level (CL) `ANY` is for writes only and ensures that the write will persist on any server in the cluster. CL `ONE` ensures that at least one server within the replica set will persist the write or respond to the read; this is the minimum consistency level for reads. CL `QUORUM` means the read/write will go to half of the nodes in the replica set plus one. CL `LOCAL_QUORUM` is like `QUORUM` but applies to only those nodes within the same data center. CL `EACH_QUORUM` is like `QUORUM` but ensures a quorum read/write on each of the data centers. CL `ALL` ensures that all nodes in a replica set will receive the read/write.

Due to the nature of quorum reads/writes, the minimum size cluster you can have, and still survive a single node outage with consistent reads/writes, is a three-node cluster with a replication factor of 3. This means that each quorum read/write goes to two nodes; the third node will be eventually consistent. This allows you to lose one node and still have consistent data.

In the event that a consistency level cannot be met (e.g., enough nodes are down that the read/write cannot be guaranteed), Cassandra will respond with an `UnavailableException`. If this happens, the application can decide to lower the consistency level and try again or handle the error state.

Our Hope

We know there is a lot to learn when diving into Cassandra. Just like any other distributed system, it can be complex. But by the end of this book, we hope to have simplified it enough for you not only to build a new application based on Cassandra but also to be able to administer the cluster supporting your application. We will walk you through building an application that will show the basics of data modeling, schema design, and common usage patterns best suited for Cassandra.

We will cover the basics of what languages are available for use with Cassandra and how to get going with some of the most common ones. This book is geared toward people who are looking to get up and running on Cassandra quickly. The goal is to keep to the facts and mentalities that will enable you to design and build your own applications and administer your own clusters as quickly as possible.

2

Installation

Cassandra is a Java application at its core. Because of this, there are certain considerations that need to be taken into account when installing it. This chapter will highlight the different installation types for the base binary and packages. We will go over the important configuration items and files. Then, once Cassandra is installed, we will dive into setting up single- and multinode clusters, assigning the proper tokens for a cluster, and then ensuring that our cluster is up and running.

Prerequisites

Cassandra requires the most stable release of Java 1.6. While it may run on Java 1.7, it has not been fully tested and vetted for that version. If you are running multiple versions of Java on a single system, set the `JAVA_HOME` variable to the path of the 1.6 version and add 1.6 to the beginning of the user's `PATH`.

There are several directories that you should be aware of when installing Cassandra. The data directories contain the SSTable files for all ColumnFamilys. This folder defaults to /var/lib/cassandra/data. The data directories should be on a separate volume from the system volume. The CommitLog directories store Cassandra's append-only data; the default directory for the CommitLog is /var/lib/cassandra/commitlog. This volume should not reside on the same volume as the system or the data directory. The CommitLog relies on the performance of append-only files, and doing random seeks during append-only writes will greatly affect the write performance. The saved cache's default directory is located in /var/lib/cassandra/saved_caches. This directory is where the key/row caches get saved for faster loading on start-up. By default, Cassandra writes all of its logs to /var/log/cassandra. All directories need to be writable by the user who is running Cassandra.

Installation

Installation coverage includes installation from Debian and RedHat/CentOS/Oracle packages and from binaries.

Debian

Add the following to /etc/apt/sources.list.d/cassandra.sources.list:

```
deb http://debian.datastax.com/community stable main
```

Install DataStax Community:

```
curl -L http://debian.datastax.com/debian/repo_key | sudo apt-key add -
sudo apt-get update
sudo apt-get install dsc12
```

The Cassandra service will start automatically.

RedHat/CentOS/Oracle

Make sure you have EPEL (Extra Packages for Enterprise Linux) installed:

```
rpm -Uvh http://dl.fedoraproject.org/pub/epel/5/i386/epel-release-5-4.noarch.rpm
```

Add a Yum repository for DataStax in /etc/yum.repos.d/datastax.repo:

```
[datastax]
  name= DataStax Repo for Apache Cassandra
  baseurl=http://rpm.datastax.com/community
  enabled=1
gpgcheck=0
```

Install DataStax Community using Yum:

```
yum install dsc12
```

Start DataStax Community (as a single-node cluster):

```
sudo dsc cassandra
```

From Binaries

Download the .tar archive:

```
curl -OL http://downloads.datastax.com/community/dsc.tar.gz
```

Unpack the .tar archive for DataStax Community:

```
tar -xzvf dsc.tar.gz
```

Go to the install directory:

```
cd dsc-cassandra-1.2.x
```

Start DataStax Community from the install directory:

```
sudo bin/cassandra
```

Configuration

The Cassandra configuration files, by default, are kept in the conf directory in the application path, or if you install via the .deb or .rpm packages, they will be in the /etc/cassandra directory.

The cassandra.yaml file contains most of the configuration items required to successfully set up a Cassandra cluster. The following list describes each of the most important options in the cassandra.yaml file and their defaults:

- **`cluster_name`**
  Default: "Test Cluster." The name of this cluster. The name of the cluster determines which cluster a node will belong to and prevents the node from joining an unwanted cluster by mistake.
- **`num_tokens`**
  Default: 256. The number of tokens randomly assigned to this node. When virtual nodes (vnodes) are used, this tells Cassandra how much data, in proportion to the cluster, this node owns. Given a three-node cluster, if one node has ten tokens and the other two have five tokens, the node with ten tokens will own 50% of the data in the entire cluster. One may want to do this when using commodity hardware that may not all be the same.
- **`initial_token`**
  Default: blank. When vnodes are not being used, or there is only one token per node, the initial token specifies where in the range this node belongs. If this field is left blank, Cassandra will try to determine which nodes in the cluster have the largest load, and it will bisect the range of those nodes. If Cassandra cannot determine which nodes have the highest load, it will select a random token. Because of this, when setting up a new cluster, it is important to manually calculate the tokens for each node that will be in the cluster.
- **`authenticator`**
  Default: org.apache.cassandra.auth.AllowAllAuthenticator. This chooses the Java class used for authentication with Cassandra. By default, there is no authentication for a node in Cassandra. Optionally, you may specify org.apache.cassandra.auth.Password Authenticator. That will keep usernames and hashed passwords in the system_auth.credentials table. It is recommended to use a replication factor of 2 or higher when using the PasswordAuthenticator to prevent data loss in the event of an outage.
- **`authorizer`**
  Default: org.apache.cassandra.auth.AllowAllAuthorizer. This chooses the Java class responsible for limiting and granting permissions to Cassandra objects. By default, the AllowAllAuthorizer turns off authorization. Optionally, the CassandraAuthorizer may be used, in which case the permissions will be stored in the system_auth .permissions table.

- **permissions_validity_in_ms**
Default: 2000. When using the Authorizer, this specifies how long to cache permissions. If permissions do not change very often, increase this value to increase the read/write performance. This is ignored when using the AllowAllAuthorizer.

- **partitioner**
Default: org.apache.cassandra.dht.Murmur3Partitioner. This specifies the Java class that is responsible for partitioning the data among the nodes. The Murmur3Partitioner is an extremely fast hash-based partitioner for random distribution. Optionally, one may also choose the ByteOrderedPartitioner, which orders the keys by their byte value, or the CollatingOPP, which orders based on the U.S. English value. It is important to note that when using the ordered partitioners, the ability to do range slices is given but may also lead to hot spots. If you change this parameter, you will destroy all data in the data directories.

- **data_file_directories**
Default: /var/lib/cassandra/data. Where Cassandra should store the data on disk.

- **commitlog_directory**
Default: /var/lib/cassandra/commitlog. Where Cassandra should store the CommitLogs. This value should reside on a different volume from the `data_file_directories`.

- **disk_failure_policy**
Default: `stop`. When a disk fails, Cassandra can react differently depending on need. By default, Cassandra will stop Gossip and Thrift on the node, leaving it effectively dead. Optionally, you may specify `best_effort`, which will attempt to use the remaining good disks. The `best_effort` option is best when used with JBoD ("just a bunch of disks") configurations. You may also specify `ignore`, which will respond with a failure when attempting to access the node.

- **saved_caches_directory**
Default: /var/lib/cassandra/saved_caches. Specifies the directory in which to store the saved caches.

- **commitlog_sync**
Default: `periodic`. By default, Cassandra will acknowledge writes immediately, then periodically fsync those writes to disk. Optionally, if `batch` is specified, Cassandra will not acknowledge writes until the batch has been fsynced.

- **commitlog_sync_period_in_ms**
Default: 10000. Specifies the time in which Cassandra will fsync writes to disk. When using batch syncs, this value should be low as writes will block until the sync happens.

- **commitlog_segment_size_in_mb**
Default: 32. This specifies how large the CommitLog will grow before a new file is created.

- **seed_provider**
Default: org.apache.cassandra.locator.SimpleSeedProvider. Specifies the Java class that will provide the seeds that will allow nodes to autodetect the cluster. The SimpleSeedProvider by default takes a parameter of seeds, which is a comma-delimited list of nodes to act as

seed nodes. When running a multiple-node cluster, it is important to have as many seeds as possible so new nodes will be able to bootstrap in the event of an outage of a seed node.

- **concurrent_reads**
  Default: 32. The number of concurrent reads that are allowed to take place. Because heavy read loads can pull large amounts of data from disk, the reads are going to be I/O bound. A general rule of thumb is to set this value to 16 * the number of disks in use by data_file_directories.
- **concurrent_writes**
  Default: 32. The number of concurrent writes. Because writes are appended to the CommitLog, they are almost never I/O bound. The general rule of thumb for concurrent writes is 16 * the number of cores in the machine.
- **memtable_total_space_in_mb**
  Default: not specified. When specified, Cassandra will flush the largest MemTable when this limit has been reached. When left unspecified, Cassandra will flush the largest MemTable when it reaches one-third of the heap.
- **listen_address**
  Default: localhost. This is the address that the host listens on. When left unspecified, the listen address will default to the local address. In most cases, this will work. If left at localhost, other nodes may not be able to communicate.

Cluster Setup

Simply installing the package and running Cassandra will run a single-node cluster. The default configuration options will all be suitable with the exception of listen_address, which needs to be changed from localhost in order to take external connections.

Multinode clusters are slightly more complex to set up as the new nodes need to know about the existing nodes in the cluster. New Cassandra nodes discover information about the other nodes via a protocol called Gossip. To get everything working correctly, we will need to modify a few of the configuration options to ensure that Gossip will be able to communicate properly and to ensure that your data is distributed properly.

When bringing a new node into the cluster, you must specify a "seed node." The seed nodes are a set of nodes that are used to give information about the cluster to newly joining nodes. The seed nodes should be stable and should also point to other seed nodes; that is, there should be no single seed node that will point to itself as the seed node. The seed nodes are specified in the partitioner section of the configuration file.

The second option to specify is the initial_token. A token represents a node's place in the cluster, as well as how much data that node is supposed to own. The token is a number between 0 and $(2^{127}-1)$. This initial token is used only the first time the node boots, after which you will need to use nodetool move to change the token. In most situations, you will want to have a balanced cluster, where every node owns the same amount of data. When creating a balanced cluster, the formula to create the tokens is $2^{\wedge 127}/K * N$, where K is the total number of nodes in the cluster and N is the number of the nodes you are calculating for based on a zero index. Listing 2.1 shows pseudo code representing how to generate tokens for a six-node cluster.

Listing 2.1 **Pseudo Code to Print Out Even Tokens in a Six-Node Cluster**

```
NODES=6
for each n in 0 to NODES :
 token = 2^127 / NODES * n
 print token
```

Once the cluster is up and running, you can use the command-line tool `nodetool` to show various statistics about the nodes in the cluster. The option for `nodetool` to describe the ring, its tokens, load, and the effective ownership of the nodes in the cluster is `nodetool ring`. Just run the command from any node in the ring to get an output of the entire ring's statistics. Listing 2.2 shows the usage of `nodetool ring` and example output for a six-node cluster.

Listing 2.2 **Using `nodetool` to Show Cluster State**

```
$ nodetool ring
Address         DC              Rack      Status         State       Load Owns     Token
141784319550391026443072753096570088105
127.0.0.1      datacenter1     rack1     Up Normal      6.82 KB     16.67%        0
127.0.0.2      datacenter1     rack1     Up Normal      9.09 KB     16.67%
28356863910078205288614550619314017621
127.0.0.3      datacenter1     rack1     Up Normal      13.5 KB     16.67%
56713727820156410577229101238628035242
127.0.0.4      datacenter1     rack1 Up Normal          15.57 KB    16.67%
85070591730234615865843651857942052863
127.0.0.5      datacenter1     rack1     Up Normal      13.52 KB    16.67%
113427455640312821154458202477256070484
127.0.0.6      datacenter1     rack1     Up Normal      6.82 KB     16.67%
141784319550391026443072753096570088105
```

Summary

Installing Cassandra is made easier by the use of common package management systems. While the default configuration options will get you up and running, it is important to know each of the configuration options available and what they mean. In this chapter, we discussed only the basic, most commonly used configuration options. Chapter 6, "Performance Tuning," will go deeper into the configuration options and how to use each of them to get the best performance out of your Cassandra cluster.

3

Data Modeling

When creating a data model for your keyspace, the most important thing to do is to forget everything you know about relational data modeling. Relational data models are designed for efficient storage, relational lookups, and associations between concerns. The Cassandra data model is designed for raw performance and storage of vast amounts of data.

Unlike relational databases, the data model for Cassandra is based on the query patterns required. This means that you have to know the read/write patterns before you create your data model. This also applies to indexes. Indexes in Cassandra are a requirement for specific types of queries, unlike a relational database where indexes are a performance-tuning device.

In this chapter, we will highlight some key differences between creating a relational model and a Cassandra model. We will then dive into an example data model for storing time-series data.

The Cassandra Data Model

To understand how to model in Cassandra, you must first understand how the Cassandra data model works. Cassandra gets its data distribution from the Dynamo whitepaper by Amazon and its data representation from the BigTable whitepaper by Google.

When creating a table using CQL, you are not only telling Cassandra what the name and type of data are, you are also telling it how to store and distribute your data. This is done via the `PRIMARY KEY` operator. The `PRIMARY KEY` tells the Cassandra storage system to distribute the data based on the value of this key; this is known as a partition key. When there are multiple fields in the `PRIMARY KEY`, as is the case with compound keys, the first field is the partition key (how the data is distributed) and the subsequent fields are known as the clustering keys (how the data is stored on disk). Clustering keys allow you to pregroup your data by the values in the keys. Using compound keys in Cassandra is commonly referred to as "wide rows." "Wide rows" refers to the rows that Cassandra is storing on disk, rather than the rows that are represented to you when you make a query.

Figure 3.1 shows how the data in Listing 3.1 might be stored in a five-node cluster.

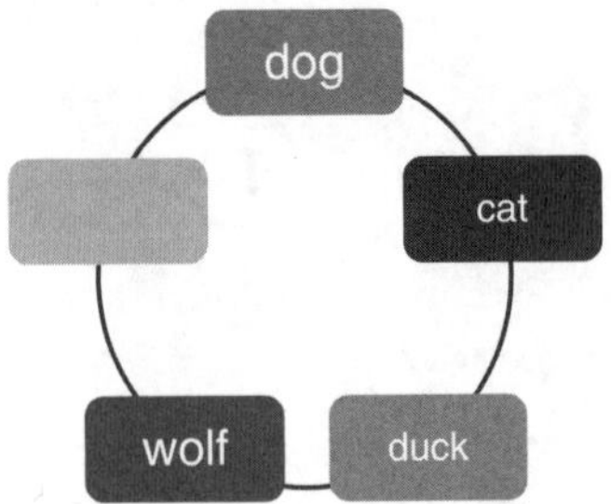

Figure 3.1 Illustration of how data may be stored using a PRIMARY KEY

Listing 3.1 **Illustration of How Data May Be Stored Using a Single** PRIMARY KEY

```
CREATE TABLE animals (
 name TEXT PRIMARY KEY,
 species TEXT,
 subspecies TEXT,
 genus TEXT,
 family TEXT
);
SELECT * FROM animals;
name  |family    | genus | species           | subspecies
------+----------+-------+-------------------+------------------
 dog  | Canidae  | Canis |          C. lupus | C. l. familiaris
 cat  | Felidae  | Felis |          F. catus |             null
 duck | Anatidae |  Anas | A. platyrhynchos  |             null
 wolf | Canidae  | Canis |          C. lupus |             null
```

Figure 3.2 shows how the data in Listing 3.2 might be stored in a five-node cluster using a COMPOUND KEY.

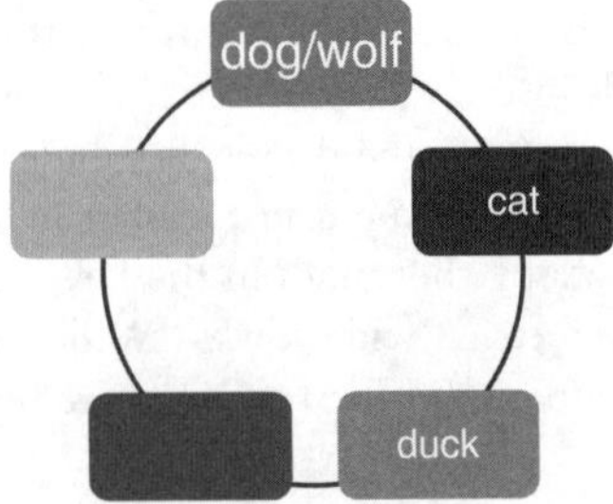

Figure 3.2 Illustration of how data may be stored using a COMPOUND KEY

Listing 3.2 **Illustration of How Data May Be Stored Using a `COMPOUND KEY`**

```
CREATE TABLE animals (
 name TEXT,
 species TEXT,
 subspecies TEXT,
 genus TEXT,
 family TEXT,
 PRIMARY KEY(family, genus)
);
SELECT * FROM animals;
name  | family   | genus | species           | subspecies
------+----------+-------+-------------------+------------------
  dog |  Canidae | Canis |          C. lupus | C. l. familiaris
 wolf |  Canidae | Canis |          C. lupus |             null
  cat |  Felidae | Felis |          F. catus |             null
 duck | Anatidae |  Anas | A. platyrhynchos  |             null
```

As you can see in Figure 3.2, when we use a `COMPOUND KEY`, the data for wolf and for dog is stored on the same server. This is because we changed the partition to "family" and clustered on "genus." Literally, this means that the data for each family will be stored on the same replica sets and presorted, or clustered, by the genus. This will allow for very fast lookups when the family and genus for an animal are known.

Model Queries—Not Data

The first thing you should consider when creating a data model in Cassandra is the performance characteristics of the query patterns. In Cassandra, rows are not segmented across nodes. This means that if a row exists on a node, the entire row will exist on that node. If you have a heavy read or write load on a particular key, this can lead to hot spots. Hot spots occur when a particular key (row) gets so many queries that it causes the load on the machine to spike. High load on a given machine can cause cluster-wide complications as the communication channels start to back up. Consideration also needs to be given to the row size. A single row has to fit on disk; if you have a single row containing billions of columns, it may extend past the amount of available disk space on the drive.

In Listing 3.3, you can see a typical way to store event logs in a relational database. There is an atomically incrementing ID field, an event time, an event type ID that relates to an event type, and some information about the event. While you may be able to mimic this model in Cassandra, it would not be performant and would cause queries that would require two lookups (one for the event row and the other for the event type), as Cassandra does not support joins.

Listing 3.3 **Example of a Relational Data Model for Log Storage**

```
CREATE TABLE events (
 id INT PRIMARY KEY,
 time TIME,
```

(Continues)

Listing 3.3 **Example of a Relational Data Model for Log Storage *(continued)***

```
 event_type INT references event_types(id),
 data text
);
SELECT * FROM events;
id |        time       | event_type |       data
.......+.......................+................+......................
 1 | 16:41:33.90814 |          4 | some event data
 2 |  16:59:48.9131 |          2 | some event data
 3 | 17:12:12.12758 |          4 | some event data
 4 | 17:32:17.83765 |          1 | some event data
 5 | 17:48:57.10934 |          0 | some event data
```

To get around the lack of joins, we can just store the `event_type` value in the column every time. This denormalization of data is certainly not frowned upon when using Cassandra. Modeling for Cassandra should follow the idea that disk space is cheap, so duplicating data (even multiple times) should not be an issue. In fact, "normalization" of data is an anti-pattern in Cassandra. The Cassandra model would be similar; however, there are a few key differences that will make a world of difference in performance and usability.

Listing 3.4 shows an exact copy of the relational version, but storing each event type as the value rather than the ID of a relation. The primary concern with this model is that each row has a single event. This makes it very difficult to find events that belong to a particular time or event type. Basically, you have to know the ID of the event to get its information without doing a full scan of the ColumnFamily.

Listing 3.4 **Example of Cassandra Data Model for Log Storage (Copy of RDBMS)**

```
CREATE TABLE events (
 id UUID PRIMARY KEY,
 time TIMESTAMP,
 event_type TEXT,
 data text
);
```

We can solve some of the issues here with indexes; however, the code would not be as performant as it could be. Let's say you would like to get all events for a particular hour. We can easily add an index to the `time` field, but this will cause excessive load, as every event will need to be pulled from different rows scattered about the cluster.

To compensate for this, since we know the hour we want ahead of time, we can key off that, and by using dynamic tables in Cassandra, we can ensure that every event for that particular hour exists, physically, on the same row. When you specify multiple fields in the `PRIMARY KEY`, Cassandra will key off the first field and every subsequent field will be a part of the column name. In Listing 3.5, we restructure the code to store fields by hour in the table to make hourly lookups of events easier.

Listing 3.5 **Example of Cassandra Data Model for Log Storage (Low Traffic)**

```
CREATE TABLE events (
 hour TIMESTAMP,
 id UUID,
 time TIMESTAMP,
 event_type TEXT,
 data text
 PRIMARY KEY(hour, id)
);
```

With this new model, we can look up all events from a single hour easily as we can ensure that everything that happened within that hour exists in a single row on disk. This may be a perfectly suitable model for a low-volume application. However, if you have heavy reads and/or writes, you may need to segment the row into multiple rows. Seeing as an event per row is difficult to query, and a row every hour can lead to hot spots, as all reads and writes are going to the same files on disk, we can segment the row into multiple rows that are easy to read as long as we have a piece of information to query by; in this case, it is `event_type`. We can further improve performance by ensuring that the order is stored by event time rather than ID. This will make it possible to do range queries based on the time of an event, without scanning the entire row. In Listing 3.6, we will use a composite row key and clustering order to remove hot spots and order by event time in a descending fashion.

Listing 3.6 **Example of Cassandra Data Model for Log Storage (Optimized)**

```
CREATE TABLE events (
 hour TIMESTAMP,
 id TIMEUUID,
 time TIMESTAMP,
 event_type TEXT,
 data text,
 PRIMARY KEY((hour, event_type), time)
) WITH CLUSTERING ORDER BY (time DESC);
SELECT * FROM events;
hour                | event_type | time                | data      | id
--------------------+------------+---------------------+-----------+-----
2013-06-13 11:00:00 |      click | 2013-06-13 11:00:00 | some data | 3...
2013-06-13 11:00:00 |  page_view | 2013-06-13 11:00:01 | some data | 2...
2013-06-13 11:00:00 |      error | 2013-06-13 11:00:05 | some data | 0...
2013-06-13 11:00:00 |   redirect | 2013-06-13 11:00:09 | some data | 1...
```

Now that we have a mechanism for storing our raw events, we may also want to track metrics around the events. Cassandra does not have the ability to create aggregate metrics in an ad hoc manner. In order to track specific aggregate information, we first need to know what aggregate metrics we would like to track. In this example, we will track event types by hour. A good candidate for this type of tracking is Cassandra counter columns. Listing 3.7 shows the table creation for a counter ColumnFamily.

Listing 3.7 Example of Counter Column Table Creation

```
CREATE TABLE event_metrics (
 hour TIMESTAMP,
 event_type TEXT,
 count COUNTER,
 PRIMARY KEY(hour, event_type)
);
CREATE TABLE url_metrics (
 hour TIMESTAMP,
 url TEXT,
 count COUNTER,
 PRIMARY KEY(hour, url)
);
```

Now that we have created the tables for `event_metrics` that contain our counters, we can update the counters at the same time using a `BATCH` statement. Listing 3.8 shows the insertion of the raw event and updating of the counters in a single atomic batch.

Listing 3.8 Example of Using an Atomic Counter BATCH to Insert and Update

```
 INSERT INTO events (hour, id, time, event_type, data)
    VALUES ('2013-06-13 11:00:00', NOW(), '2013-06-13 11:43:23',
        'click', '{"url":"http://example.com"}')
BEGIN COUNTER BATCH
 UPDATE event_metrics SET count = count + 1
  WHERE hour = '2013-06-13 11:00:00'
   AND event_type = 'click'
 UPDATE url_metrics SET count = count + 1
  WHERE hour = '2013-06-13 11:00:00'
   AND url = 'http://example.com'
APPLY BATCH;
```

Collections

Cassandra also includes collections as part of its data model. Collections are a complex type that can provide flexibility in querying.

Sets

Cassandra sets provide a means of keeping a unique set of items without the need for read-before-write. This means that one can easily solve the problem of tracking unique e-mail addresses or unique IP addresses. Lists are ordered by the natural order of the type selected. Listing 3.9 shows how to create a table with a set type and query it.

Listing 3.9 **Example of Using a Set**

```
CREATE TABLE users (
 email TEXT PRIMARY KEY,
 portfolios SET@UUID:,
 tickers SET@TEXT:
);
UPDATE users
  SET portfolios = portfolios + {756716f7-2e54-4715-9f00-91dcbea6cf50},
    tickers = tickers + {'AMZN'}
 WHERE email = 'foo@bar.com';
UPDATE users
  SET portfolios = portfolios + {756716f7-2e54-4715-9f00-91dcbea6cf50},
    tickers = tickers + {'GOOG'}
 WHERE email = 'foo@bar.com';

 email       | portfolios                             | tickers
-------------+----------------------------------------+------------------
 foo@bar.com | {756716f7-2e54-4715-9f00-91dcbea6cf50} | {'AMZN', 'GOOG'}
UPDATE users
  SET tickers = tickers - {'AMZN'}
 WHERE email = 'foo@bar.com';
 email       | portfolios                             | tickers
-------------+----------------------------------------+------------------
 foo@bar.com | {756716f7-2e54-4715-9f00-91dcbea6cf50} | {'GOOG'}
DELETE tickers
 FROM users
 WHERE email = 'foo@bar.com';
 email       | portfolios                             | tickers
-------------+----------------------------------------+------------------
 foo@bar.com | {756716f7-2e54-4715-9f00-91dcbea6cf50} | null
```

Lists

When uniqueness is not required, and maintaining order is required, Cassandra lists come in handy. Let's say we want to allow our users to specify the top five tickers from the previous example. Listing 3.10 shows an example of lists.

Listing 3.10 **Example of Using Lists**

```
ALTER TABLE users ADD top_tickers list<text>;
UPDATE users
  SET top_tickers = ['GOOG']
 WHERE email = 'foo@bar.com';
UPDATE users
  SET top_tickers = top_tickers + ['AMZN']
 WHERE email = 'foo@bar.com';
email        | portfolios            | tickers | top_tickers
-------------+-----------------------+---------+------------------
 foo@bar.com | {756716f7-2e54... }   |    null | ['GOOG', 'AMZN']
```

(Continues)

Listing 3.10 **Example of Using Lists *(continued)***

```
UPDATE users
  SET top_tickers[1] = 'FB'
WHERE email = 'foo@bar.com';
 email       | portfolios           | tickers | top_tickers
-------------+----------------------+---------+---------------
 foo@bar.com | {756716f7-2e54...}   |    null | ['GOOG', 'FB']
UPDATE users
  SET top_tickers = top_tickers - ['FB']
 WHERE email = 'foo@bar.com';
 email       | portfolios           | tickers | top_tickers
-------------+----------------------+---------+---------------
 foo@bar.com | {756716f7-2e54...}   |    null | ['GOOG']
```

Maps

Cassandra maps provide a dictionary-like object with keys and values. Maps are useful when you want to store table-like data within a single Cassandra row. This can help eliminate the pain of not having joins, or remove the need to store JSON data within a single column value. Listing 3.11 shows an example of using maps.

Listing 3.11 **Example of Using Maps**

```
ALTER TABLE users ADD ticker_updates map<text, timestamp>;
UPDATE users
  SET ticker_updates = { 'AMZN':'2013-06-13 11:42:12' }
 WHERE email = 'foo@bar.com';
email          | portfolios      | ticker_updates
---------------+-----------------+-----------------------------------------
 foo@bar.com | {756716f7...}     | {'AMZN': '2013-06-13 11:42:12-0400'}
UPDATE users
  SET ticker_updates['GOOG'] = '2013-06-13 12:51:31'
 WHERE email = 'foo@bar.com';
email          | portfolios      | ticker_updates
---------------+-----------------+-----------------------------------------
 foo@bar.com | {756716f7... }    | {'AMZN': '2013-06-13 11:42:12-0400',
                                    'GOOG': '2013-06-13 12:51:31-0400'}
DELETE ticker_updates['AMZN']
 FROM users
 WHERE email = 'foo@bar.com';
email          | portfolios      | ticker_updates
---------------+-----------------+-----------------------------------------
 foo@bar.com | {756716f7...}     | {'GOOG': '2013-06-13 12:51:31-0400'}
```

Summary

Data modeling in Cassandra may seem counterintuitive to someone who is used to a relational database. Certain concessions need to be made to gain performance in high-volume workloads. The main points to take away from this chapter are that relational database modeling techniques will almost never apply; model your queries, not your data; and denormalization and duplication of data are not bad—in fact, they are recommended. Also, keep in mind that "normalization" of your data, in any way, is almost never recommended. Collections can be very powerful, but they may impact performance when it comes to very large data sets.

4

CQL

Due to the complex data structures that Cassandra has to offer, it is critical that there be a simple way to manipulate the data you have stored. SQL seemed to be the obvious choice, but there are many things that SQL offers in the way of RDBMSs that Cassandra just cannot yet do.

Enter CQL. Cassandra Query Language (CQL) strives to be as close to SQL as possible. Given that Cassandra is a nonrelational database, a fully featured SQL construct is not possible. The main thing to note about CQL is that it has no concept of `GROUP` or `JOIN`, and a very limited implementation of `ORDER BY`.

This chapter will focus on data creation and manipulation using CQL 3. We will show the parallels of CQL with other features of Cassandra and show the end-result data structures that are created when defining different CQL schemas. We will first discuss the differences between the major versions of CQL and how they represent the underlying data structures. We will then start our focus on CQL 3, moving from data types to available commands, usage, and finally to example data structures and their correlation to Cassandra storage mechanisms.

A Familiar Way of Doing Things

Before CQL there was Thrift. Thrift is a multilanguage Remote Procedure Call (RPC) layer that was designed to make client integration as easy as wrapping a library. As the complexity of Cassandra grew, more and more client drivers started falling behind in new feature implementation. CQL arose out of the need for a server-side API that would make keeping up with client drivers much easier and require less frequent updates.

CQL 1

CQL 1 was a very basic implementation. It had the ability to create ColumnFamilys and indexes and to select and insert data. It did not have support for composite columns, wide rows, or other advanced data types.

The tokens used in the query language were the same as those used in the Thrift client. This made it easy to move from Thrift to CQL, as the ideas were the same, just expressed in an SQL-like statement.

CQL 2

CQL 2 is often referred to as "a language for wide rows." CQL 2 filled in the gaps that CQL 1 had. This meant that one could create a wide-row ColumnFamily and access it using CQL. Arguably the most used and most important feature of Cassandra is the ability to get a slice of columns from a row. This enables a user to create very wide rows where the column name may not be known ahead of time.

In many ways, CQL 2 was just an SQL-like syntax of the Thrift API representation of data. This meant the user still had to be aware of the underlying data structures and concepts that come along with storing data in Cassandra. This made CQL 2 easy to implement for current Cassandra users as it mapped directly to the storage engine. There were, however, many problems with this.

Because the number of columns returned was indefinite, there had to be two `LIMIT` clauses, one for the row limit and another for the column limit. This created several issues when there could be different column counts in rows. Functions like `COUNT` would not work either, for the same reason. As a result, `COUNT` was never implemented. You also could not specify indexes on wide rows because of the underlying limitation that indexes could only be on predefined columns. Since the columns are not defined ahead of time, there is no way to specify an index for them. Also, if you were using CompositeType columns in your wide rows, the column names needed to be unpacked manually. This led to the clients' or the applications' needing to know the composite packing structure for CQL.

CQL 3

CQL 3 compensates for the shortcomings of the previous versions by actually transposing the wide rows and unpacking them into named columns. This means that many rows can be visualized via CQL 3 from a single physical row in the data structure. CQL 3 can accomplish this by attaching metadata to the ColumnFamily and to each row.

Since CQL 3 has special metadata attached, this presents a problem for backward compatibility with legacy tables. All of your current tables already exist in the CQL 3 space as `COMPACT STORAGE` or legacy tables. In CQL 3, the `PRIMARY KEY` determines whether a ColumnFamily is static or dynamic. A static ColumnFamily will have a single `PRIMARY KEY`, while a dynamic ColumnFamily will have a compound `PRIMARY KEY`. When creating a dynamic ColumnFamily, the first part of the compound `PRIMARY KEY` is known as the partition key. In the Thrift API, this maps directly to the row key. Each subsequent part of the compound `PRIMARY KEY` is the column's name. If there are more than two parts to the `PRIMARY KEY`, the column name becomes a column of CompositeType and each of the parts after the partition key is a part of the composite. CQL 3 uses this information to generate the rows with proper column names.

Data Types

CQL 3 supports many data types, including all data types available to Cassandra. Table 4.1 shows the supported data types and their associated meanings.

Table 4.1 **CQL 3 Data Types**

Type	Description
`ascii`	ASCII character string.
`bigint`	64-bit signed `long`.
`blob`	Arbitrary bytes (no validation).
`boolean`	True or false.
`counter`	Counter column (64-bit signed value). See the "Counters" section for details.
`decimal`	Variable-precision decimal.
`double`	64-bit IEEE 754 floating point.
`float`	32-bit IEEE 754 floating point.
`inet`	An IP address. It can be either 4 bytes long (IPv4) or 16 bytes long (IPv6). There is no `inet` constant; IP addresses should be inputted as strings.
`int`	32-bit signed `int`.
`text`	UTF-8 encoded string.
`timestamp`	A timestamp. Timestamps can be entered as either a string date or an integer as the number of milliseconds since the UNIX epoch (January 1, 1970, UTC).
`timeuuid`	Type 1 UUID. This is generally used as a "conflict-free" timestamp.
`uuid`	Type 1 or type 4 UUID.
`varchar`	UTF-8 encoded string.
`varint`	Arbitrary-precision integer.

Dates

When using the `Date` type in Cassandra, you can specify the timestamp as either an integer representation of milliseconds since the UNIX epoch, or one of several variations on the ISO 8601 date format. Here are a few examples of proper dates, all showing the date June 13, 2013:

- `1371081600000`
- `2013-06-13 00:00+0000`
- `2013-06-13 00:00:00+0000`
- `2013-06-13T00:00+0000`
- `2013-06-13T00:00:00+0000`
- `2013-06-13 00:00`
- `2013-06-13 00:00:00`
- `2013-06-13T00:00`
- `2013-06-13T00:00:00`
- `2013-06-13`
- `2013-06-13+0000`

It is important to note that when the time zone is omitted, the time zone used will be the one that is configured for that particular Cassandra node. This could have implications for data centers that are configured in different time zones. When the time is omitted, the time of 00:00:00 will be used in its place.

Counters

When working with counters, it is very important to note that you cannot create a table with columns that have a type of `counter` mixed with any other type. Tables created for counters are physically separate from other types of tables. The `counter` type may not be set; you can increment or decrement the counter only by a specified amount. Counters may not be part of the `PRIMARY KEY` of the table.

TimeUUID

`TimeUUID` types have a few extra functions that allow you to extract the time information from the `TimeUUID` object.

now()

The `now` function when executed will return a new `TimeUUID` with the time of the current timestamp; this ensures that the `TimeUUID` created is globally unique and contains the current time when the statement was executed. This statement is effectively useless for `WHERE` clauses.

minTimeuuid() and maxTimeuuid()

The `minTimeuuid` and `maxTimeuuid` functions are used when querying ranges of `TimeUUID`s by their embedded time. When using these methods, it is important to note that they do *not* generate RFC-4122-compliant UUIDs. This means that the values returned are not guaranteed to be globally unique and therefore should be used only when querying data and never for inserting data. The functions take a parameter that is compatible with the timestamp type. See Listing 4.1 for example usage.

Listing 4.1 **Example Usage of `minTimeuuid()` and `maxTimeuuid()`**

```
SELECT *
 FROM events
WHERE event_time > maxTimeuuid('2013-01-01 00:05+0000')
  AND event_time < minTimeuuid('2013-02-02 10:00+0000')
```

dateOf() and unixTimestampOf()

The `dateOf` and `unixTimestampOf` functions take an argument of `TimeUUID` and return the timestamp in it. The `dateOf` method will return a type of `timestamp`, whereas the `unixTimestampOf` method will return a `bigint` that is representative of the number of milliseconds since the UNIX epoch.

Commands

CQL 3 supports a subset of the SQL commands. In the following sections, we will describe the commands that are currently supported and show example usage of each one.

CREATE/ALTER KEYSPACE

`CREATE KEYSPACE` (Listing 4.2) and `ALTER KEYSPACE` are used to add or modify top-level strategy options for a collection of tables. When creating a keyspace, the keyspace name must be alphanumeric with a length of 32 or less. There are two supported properties for the `CREATE/ALTER KEYSPACE` commands, `replication` and `durable_writes`. When specifying `replication`, you may choose one of two options, SimpleStrategy and NetworkTopologyStrategy. SimpleStrategy will create a replication factor that is consistent across the entire cluster, and the only option available is the `replication_factor`, which must be defined. NetworkTopologyStrategy allows you to decide the replication factor for each individual data center. The `durable_writes` option specifies whether or not to use the CommitLog when writing data. This is on by default and should not be turned off as data loss could result in the event of an outage.

Listing 4.2 **Example Usage of** `CREATE KEYSPACE`

```
CREATE KEYSPACE Analytics
WITH replication = {'class': 'SimpleStrategy', 'replication_factor' : 3};
CREATE KEYSPACE Analytics
WITH replication = {'class': 'NetworkTopologyStrategy', 'west' : 1, 'east' : 3}
AND durable_writes = false;
```

USE

The `USE` statement (Listing 4.3) switches the keyspace from the one you are working in. This works exactly like the `USE` statement in SQL.

Listing 4.3 **Example Usage of** `USE`

```
USE Analytics;
```

DROP KEYSPACE

The `DROP KEYSPACE` command (Listing 4.4) works exactly like the SQL `DROP DATABASE` command. This operation is irreversible and removes all information within the specified keyspace.

Listing 4.4 **Example Usage of** `DROP KEYSPACE`

```
DROP KEYSPACE Analytics;
```

CREATE TABLE/COLUMNFAMILY

The `CREATE TABLE` statement creates a table. A table is defined as a collection of rows and columns. `CREATE COLUMNFAMILY` is an alias for `CREATE TABLE`.

Primary Keys

The `PRIMARY KEY` in the table definition defines the physical key in the underlying Cassandra data structure. Because of this, the `PRIMARY KEY` must be defined in the column definitions. Other than this, the syntax is similar to the corresponding SQL syntax. When defining the `PRIMARY KEY`, if you decide to use a compound key, only the first part of the key will be used as the underlying row key. This is called the partition key. If you want to have a composite partition key, this is defined by adding a set of parentheses around the parts you would like to be the partition key. The remaining parts of the compound key will be used as the physical parts of the composite columns in the underlying data structure. These are called the clustering keys. The clustering keys will determine the order in which the columns are stored on disk. You can optionally specify a clustering order that will order the columns on disk and directly affect the `ORDER BY` clause. Listing 4.5 demonstrates creating a static table in CQL 3.

Listing 4.5 Example Usage of `CREATE TABLE` for a Static Table

```
CREATE TABLE users (
 email text PRIMARY KEY,
 first_name text,
 last_name text,
 password text
) WITH comment='Users information'
```

Listing 4.6 demonstrates creating a dynamic table in CQL 3 with an optional composite partition key.

Listing 4.6 Example Usage of `CREATE TABLE` for a Dynamic Table

```
CREATE TABLE events (
 event_time timestamp,
 url text,
 event_id uuid,
 network_location inet,
 event_data text
 PRIMARY KEY ((url, event_time), event_id, network_location)
) WITH compaction = { 'class' : 'LeveledCompactionStrategy' }
  AND comment='Event Data'
```

Other Options

The `CREATE TABLE` syntax allows for other options to be set. These options are purely optional and are defined as key/value pairs in a `WITH` statement after the column definition. Specifying `WITH COMPACT STORAGE` will create a legacy table that will allow you to use your existing Thrift-created tables with CQL 3. The available options are specified in Table 4.2.

Table 4.2 **Additional Options for** `CREATE TABLE` **in CQL 3**

Option	Default	Description
`comment`	none	A free-form, human-readable comment.
`read_repair_chance`	0.1	The probability with which to query extra nodes for the purpose of read repairs.
`dclocal_read_repair_chance`	0	The probability with which to query extra nodes belonging to the same data center as the read coordinator for the purpose of read repairs.
`gc_grace_seconds`	864000	Time to wait before garbage-collecting tombstones (deletion markers).
`bloom_filter_fp_chance`	0.00075	The target probability of false positives of the SSTable bloom filters. Said bloom filters will be sized to provide the probability.
`compaction`		The compaction options to use.
`compression`		The compression options to use.
`replicate_on_write`	`true`	Whether to replicate data on write. This can only be set to `false` for tables with counters values.
`caching`	`keys_only`	Whether to cache keys ("key cache") and/or rows ("row cache") for this table. Valid values are `all`, `keys_only`, `rows_only`, and `none`.

DROP TABLE

The `DROP TABLE` command (Listing 4.7) works exactly as the SQL `DROP TABLE` command does. This operation is irreversible and removes all information within the specified table, as well as the table definition itself.

Listing 4.7 **Example Usage of** `DROP TABLE`

```
DROP TABLE events;
```

TRUNCATE

The `TRUNCATE` command (Listing 4.8) works exactly as the SQL `TRUNCATE` command does. This operation is irreversible and removes all information within the specified table.

Listing 4.8 **Example Usage of** `TRUNCATE`

```
TRUNCATE events;
```

CREATE INDEX

The `CREATE INDEX` statement (Listing 4.9) creates a new secondary index for the column specified. Optionally, you can specify the index name prior to the `ON` statement. If there is existing data in the table during command execution, immediate indexing of current data will occur; after that, the indexes will automatically be updated when data is modified.

Listing 4.9 **Example Usage of** `CREATE INDEX`

```
CREATE INDEX network_location_index ON events (network_location);
```

DROP INDEX

The `DROP INDEX` statement (Listing 4.10) removes an index that was created using `CREATE INDEX`.

Listing 4.10 **Example Usage of** `DROP INDEX`

```
DROP INDEX network_location_index;
```

INSERT

The `INSERT` command (Listing 4.11) is similar to the SQL counterpart. The major difference between CQL insert and SQL insert is that CQL insert requires that the `PRIMARY KEY` be specified during statement execution.

Listing 4.11 **Example Usage of** `INSERT` **Specifying a TTL**

```
INSERT INTO events (
  event_time,
  url,
  event_id,
  network_location,
  event_data
) VALUES (
  1365977131666,
  'http://www.google.com',
  now(),
  '10.10.10.10',
  '{"browser": "Firefox"}'
) USING TTL 345600;
```

UPDATE

The UDPATE command (Listing 4.12) is similar to the SQL UPDATE command. Just as with the INSERT statement, you must specify the PRIMARY KEY as part of the UPDATE WHERE statement. In addition, the only other difference is that in CQL the UPDATE command does not check for the existence of the row; if the row does not exist, CQL will just create it. Because of this, the application can exclusively use UPDATE and not have to use INSERT when modifying data.

Listing 4.12 **Example Usage of** UPDATE **Specifying a TTL**

```
UPDATE events USING TTL 345600
SET event_id=now(),
  network_location='10.10.10.10',
  event_data='{"browser": "Firefox"}'
WHERE event_time=1365977131666
 AND url='http://www.google.com';
```

DELETE

The DELETE statement (Listing 4.13) removes columns and rows. If columns are specified after the DELETE keyword, only those columns will be removed. If no columns are specified, the entire row will be removed. Just as with the INSERT and UPDATE statements, the PRIMARY KEY must be specified.

Listing 4.13 **Example Usage of** DELETE

```
DELETE event_data
 FROM events
 WHERE event_time=1365977131666
  AND url='http://www.google.com';
```

BATCH

The BATCH statement (Listing 4.14) allows a user to specify multiple statements in one request. All statements that have the same partition key will be applied atomically.

Listing 4.14 **Example Usage of** BATCH

```
BEGIN BATCH
 UPDATE events USING TTL 345600
 SET event_id=now(),
   network_location='10.10.10.10',
   event_data='{"browser": "Firefox"}'
 WHERE event_time=1365977131666
  AND url='http://www.google.com';

 DELETE event_data
  FROM events
```

(Continues)

Listing 4.14 **Example Usage of** `BATCH` ***(continued)***

```
  WHERE event_time=1365977131666
    AND url='http://www.google.com';
APPLY BATCH;
```

SELECT

The `SELECT` statement (Listing 4.15) returns rows and columns, just as in SQL the `SELECT` statement takes parameters of fields, or a "*" that tells the statement to return all columns. It can also optionally have specified a `WHERE` clause, an `ORDER BY` clause, and a `LIMIT` clause. In addition to these clauses, there is also an optional `ALLOW FILTERING` clause.

Listing 4.15 **Example Usage of** `SELECT`

```
SELECT * FROM events;
```

WHERE

The `WHERE` clause (Listing 4.16) specifies which rows must be queried. The syntax is just like that in SQL; however, the columns specified in the `WHERE` clause must be either part of the `PRIMARY KEY` or on a column that has a secondary index specified. In addition to this, non-equality-based expressions are not supported unless the table has been created with an ordered partitioner. Last, if a compound `PRIMARY KEY` is specified, the `WHERE` clause must have the contiguous parts of the `PRIMARY KEY` specified; that is to say, if the compound key has four parts, you can use parts 1, 2, and 3 in the `WHERE` clause but not 1 and 4, or 1, 2, and 4. This is a limitation of the way the data is stored in the underlying structure.

Listing 4.16 **Example Usage of** `SELECT` **with** `WHERE`

```
SELECT *
  FROM events
 WHERE url='http://www.google.com'
   AND event_time > 1365977131666;
```

ORDER BY

The `ORDER BY` option (Listing 4.17) allows you to change the order of the returned results. Just as in SQL, it takes an option of the column name and either `ASC` or `DESC` for ascending order or descending order, respectively. If the table was created with a clustering order, the available ordering options are those specified by that order or reversed; otherwise, it is limited to the order of the clustering key.

Listing 4.17 **Example Usage of** `SELECT` **with** `ORDER BY`

```
SELECT *
  FROM events
 WHERE url='http://www.google.com'
   AND event_time > 1365977131666
ORDER BY event_id DESC;
```

LIMIT

The LIMIT option (Listing 4.18) restricts the number of rows returned to the number specified. This works exactly like its SQL counterpart.

Listing 4.18 **Example Usage of SELECT with LIMIT**

```
SELECT *
  FROM events
 LIMIT 10;
```

ALLOW FILTERING

The ALLOW FILTERING option (Listing 4.19) enables the server to actively filter the results server-side. The default behavior of the WHERE clause is to only be able to reduce fields based on the PRIMARY KEY parts or items specified by the secondary indexes. With ALLOW FILTERING you can tell the server that it can manually reduce the results by the WHERE clause as long as at least one component of the WHERE clause is specified in a secondary index. If ALLOW FILTERING is used, it can have severe performance implications in situations where a lot of rows are returned. Due to these performance implications, this option should be used with extreme caution.

Listing 4.19 **Example Usage of SELECT with ALLOW FILTERING**

```
   SELECT *
    FROM events
   WHERE url='http://www.google.com'
     AND network_location='10.10.10.10'
ALLOW FILTERING;
```

Example Schemas

To better understand how Cassandra physically stores data, we will provide a few example schemas. In these examples, we will show sample output, as CQL will give you. The alternating shaded and nonshaded rows will show you the physical rows as stored in the Cassandra subsystem. The different styles of text will show the possible node distribution in a three-node cluster using a partitioner that will evenly distribute the data.

Static Tables

Static tables in Cassandra are tables whose storage schema closely represents what is returned to the user when querying the data. These have a limited number of physical columns and are created by not specifying a compound PRIMARY KEY. In the basic users table in Listing 4.20, you can see that each physical row is returned as a logical row in CQL. In addition to that, each row resides on a different node.

Listing 4.20 **Example of Static Table Data Storage**

```
CREATE TABLE users (
  email text PRIMARY KEY,
  first_name text,
  last_name text,
  password text
);
SELECT * FROM USERS;
email               | first_name | last_name |          password
--------------------+------------+-----------+------------------
russ@example.com    |       Russ | Bradberry | acbd18db4cc2f85c
eric@example.com    |       Eric |     Lubow | a48153c2edb888f9
eddie@example.com   |     Edward |       Kim | c08992871dc02c13
john@example.com    |       John | Dougherty | 8c4e114e301c4a7d
steve@example.com   |      Steve| Knightley | a4b18d8476c6caf5
```

Dynamic Tables

Dynamic tables in Cassandra are tables that, unlike static tables, do not map one CQL row to one physical row on disk. When using a compound `PRIMARY KEY`, the storage system will create a single wide row for all the possible logical rows that belong to the partition key of the table. This allows for very fast lookups and slices of data belonging to that particular partition key and also ensures that all pieces of data related to that partition key are stored near each other on disk and on the same node. Listing 4.21 is a page-view-tracking database that tracks page views by URL and rolls them up by hour. While this could have been created as a static table, we used a compound `PRIMARY KEY` to ensure that all hour data for a particular URL is kept on the same node and close on disk. This will ensure that reads for that URL are much faster. Each physical row on disk in the Cassandra storage system maps to several logical rows in CQL.

Listing 4.21 **Example of Dynamic Table Data Storage**

```
CREATE TABLE page_view_hour_rollups (
  hour timestamp,
  url text,
  page_views bigint,
  PRIMARY KEY (url, hour)
);
SELECT * FROM page_view_hour_rollups;
url                  |                     hour | page_views
---------------------+--------------------------+-----------
http://xmpl.com/1 | 2013-06-13 00:00:00+0000 |        351
http://xmpl.com/1 | 2013-06-13 02:00:00+0000 |         43
http://xmpl.com/1 | 2013-06-13 03:00:00+0000 |        914
http://xmpl.com/2 | 2013-06-13 01:00:00+0000 |       9435
http://xmpl.com/2 | 2013-06-13 02:00:00+0000 |        183
http://xmpl.com/2 | 2013-06-13 04:00:00+0000 |         98
```

```
http://xmpl.com/3 | 2013-06-13 08:00:00+0000 |      1363
http://xmpl.com/3 | 2013-06-13 09:00:00+0000 |        64
http://xmpl.com/3 | 2013-06-13 11:00:00+0000 |       736
http://xmpl.com/4 | 2013-06-13 01:00:00+0000 |       692
http://xmpl.com/4 | 2013-06-13 04:00:00+0000 |        23
http://xmpl.com/5 | 2013-06-13 09:00:00+0000 |      1553
```

Summary

CQL has come a long way since the first version. It truly bridges the gap between the Cassandra data model and the RDBMS data model. While not all features of SQL are supported, more and more features are added with every new version of Cassandra. It is important to keep in mind that just because CQL is an SQL-like language, it is not SQL and the data should definitely not be modeled as if you were using SQL. By taking advantage of CQL's many diverse features, you can easily insert and read data that would otherwise be complicated with the Thrift RPC.

5

Deployment and Provisioning

Now that you have done a little development on the application and you have it working in a development environment, it's time to think about what your production environment is going to look like. In this chapter, we will cover the different aspects of deploying Cassandra to production. These include choosing a replication factor and a placement strategy and understanding the various partitioners available with Cassandra.

Keyspace Creation

When creating your keyspace, you need to decide on a few things: your data center layout and your replication strategy. Your data center layout is part of a greater set of considerations that get bundled into the category of replication strategy. In short, you need to answer these questions: How many copies of your data do you want, and where do you want to keep them? Much of this depends on your application and your usage patterns. We will examine some of those considerations in this chapter.

Replication Factor

Before we dive into making decisions about data center layout and strategy, we should outline what replication means. Replication is simply the process of storing copies of data in more than one place. This is done to ensure reliability and fault tolerance. The replication factor refers to the number of copies of each row that are stored. So if you have a replication factor of 3 in data center us-east, that means you have three copies of each row. It is important to note that you don't have a master set of data and then two additional copies. There is no primary or master concept with Cassandra. Having three copies of the data means that you have three copies of the data that are equally valued by the cluster.

There is really only one main rule that applies to setting a replication factor. That rule is that the replication factor should not exceed the number of nodes in the cluster. If the replication factor exceeds the number of nodes, writes are rejected. Reads continue to be served if the consistency level of the request can be met. The key takeaway here is not to paint yourself into a corner by trying to be too safe and having too many copies of your data before your data center has grown to a size where it can handle the replication factor.

Replication Strategies

In order for Cassandra to be able to determine the physical location of nodes in the cluster and their proximity to each other, it needs to know how you are planning to lay things out. There are three parts to this: the replication strategy, the snitch, and the partitioner.

For replication strategies, there are two possibilities: SimpleStrategy and NetworkTopologyStrategy.

SimpleStrategy

SimpleStrategy is to be used on an individual machine or with single-data-center clusters. As a result, it is also the default placement strategy when creating a keyspace.

The way SimpleStrategy works is mostly based on the partitioner. The first replica is placed on whichever node the partitioner tells it. All additional replicas are added to the ring in a clockwise fashion. When queries are run under SimpleStrategy, there is no location awareness. In other words, the data center and rack locations of the other nodes are not taken into account.

NetworkTopologyStrategy

The best time to use the NetworkTopologyStrategy is when you have a Cassandra deployment across multiple data centers. The strategy describes the number of replicas that should be in each data center. This number is set at keyspace creation time.

Replica Counts

There are a few things to take into account when deciding how many replicas should be in each data center. The first has to do with satisfying reads within the data center. If the read has to leave the data center for a replica in another data center, you will incur network latency, which will ultimately slow down the response time of your read query.

The other major factor to take into account when deciding the replica counts within a data center is what failure cases you are willing to accept in your application. These break down into two common scenarios:

- **Two replicas per data center.** If a single node in a replica set fails, reads that were requested with a consistency level of `ONE` will still succeed. It is generally not recommended to set a replication factor of 2 if you have fewer than four nodes in a data center.
- **Three replicas per data center.** If a single node in a replica set fails, reads that were requested with a consistency level of `LOCAL_QUORUM` will still succeed. It is generally not recommended to set a replication factor of 3 if you have fewer than six nodes in a data center.

There is also a setup that is generally termed "asymmetrical replication." This means that the number of replicas in one data center does not match the number of replicas in the other data centers. There are some very good use cases for this. For instance, if you do the majority of your reads in datacenter1 and the majority of your writes in datacenter2, having more nodes in datacenter1 to reduce read latency may be a good strategy. Another good use case would be if you have a single data center that acts as an analytics data center, using a technology such as Hadoop. This data center would have drastically different read and write patterns from the other data centers and could be configured accordingly.

Snitches

The first and most obvious question here is what is a snitch? A snitch is simply a protocol that helps map IPs to racks and data centers. In other words, it creates a topology by grouping nodes together to help determine where data is read from. As an aside, there is no need to use a snitch for writes. Writes function by being sent to the receiving node and then the receiving node blocks until the consistency level for that write operation has been met.

When a read request to Cassandra happens, the requesting application asks only one node, the coordinator node. The consistency level of the read request and the `read_repair_chance` for that ColumnFamily decide how the snitch steps in. Ultimately, only one node will send back the requested data. It is up to the snitch to determine, typically based on historical performance, which node or nodes that will be.

There are a few different possible snitches that can be used with Cassandra, and each comes with its pros and cons. We will discuss what each snitch is and what is a good use case for the snitch. It should be noted that a snitch has an effect only on the way Cassandra talks to itself. It has no bearing on client applications and their communication with Cassandra.

Snitches are configured in your cassandra.yaml file. It is extremely important to remember that all nodes in a cluster must use the same snitch. If you want to change the snitch for your cluster, you must make the change in the configuration file and then restart the entire cluster.

Simple

Taking advantage of the SimpleSnitch requires very little setup or knowledge. The reason for that is the SimpleSnitch does not know anything about the data center settings or racks. The SimpleSnitch is good for a single machine or even a single-data-center deployment. You can even think of a single data center as one zone in a cloud architecture. When you are setting the SimpleSnitch, you need to remember to put the `replication_factor=#` in your keyspace `strategy_options`.

Dynamic

Dynamic snitching is actually a layer of the snitch protocol that exists in all snitches besides the SimpleSnitch. It wraps your chosen snitch and provides an additional adaptive layer for determining the best possible read locations. However, it is possible for that adaptive layer to become counterproductive. The DynamicSnitch uses latency possibility calculations to determine the best approach. There are certain circumstances in which those calculations can take longer than the query itself. In order to avoid that, the DynamicSnitch takes a two-pronged approach. The first option is for the DynamicSnitch to use recent update statistics. The second is to calculate a score for each host and run the query based on the best score.

There are a few potential issues with the calculation of scores and update checks with regard to the DynamicSnitch. What happens if a node is in the middle of a compaction? What happens if the hardware on that node isn't as powerful as some of the other nodes (since Cassandra is made to run on commodity hardware)? What happens if a node hasn't been able to check in because the coordinator node is overloaded? What happens if there isn't any information for the snitch to use to make a decision? And even more pressing, if all necessary information exists, is using latency the best approach for determining performance capabilities?

Rack Inferring

The RackInferringSnitch works by assuming it knows the topology of your network, by the octets in a node's IP address. For instance, if you have a Cassandra node at 10.20.30.1, the RackInferringSnitch will assume the following breakdown:

10. The first octet has no special meaning.
20. The second octet is the data center octet. If there was another node at 10.30.40.1, Cassandra would assume that this node was in a different physical data center.
30. The third octet is the rack octet. Cassandra assumes that all nodes in this octet are in the same rack.
40. The final octet is the node octet.

When defining your keyspace `strategy_options`, be sure to include the second octet as the data center name for clarity.

EC2

The Ec2Snitch is for Amazon Web Services (AWS)–based deployments where the entire cluster sits within a single region. The region is then considered the data center and the availability zones are considered the racks in those data centers. For example, let's assume you have a cluster set up in the us-east-1 region. If node1 is in us-east-1a and node2 is in us-east-1b, Cassandra would consider these nodes to be in two different racks within the same data center. Node1 would be considered rack 1a and node2 would be considered rack 1b.

Since the Ec2Snitch will work only in single-region deployments, you don't have to worry about public IPs for the Cassandra nodes. It also makes your keyspace definition more straightforward. When defining the `strategy_options` for your keyspace, the EC2 region name (which was us-east in the preceding example) is what should be used as the data center name. Listing 5.1 shows an example of how to create a keyspace using the Ec2Snitch in the us-east data center.

Listing 5.1 **Keyspace Creation for the Ec2Snitch in the us-east Data Center**

```
CREATE KEYSPACE VideoStore
WITH replication = {'class': 'NetworkTopologyStrategy', 'us-east' : 3}
AND durable_writes = true;
```

Ec2MultiRegion

The Ec2MultiRegionSnitch is for use in Amazon Web Services deployments where the Cassandra cluster spans multiple regions. This snitch views data centers and racks in a similar fashion to the EcC2Snitch. Using the Ec2MultiRegionSnitch, if a node is us-east-1a, us-east is the data center and 1a is the rack name.

The major difference is in setting the IP addresses. The Ec2MultiRegionSnitch requires the use of public IPs to be able to talk across regions. When configuring your node, the `listen_address` is still set to the private IP of the node. The `broadcast_address` is set to the public IP address of the node. This allows nodes in different regions to communicate. If Cassandra determines that the nodes are within the same data center, it will switch to using the private IP address of the node, the one that was set as the `listen_address`, when doing intra-availability-zone communication.

There are a few other important settings that need to be changed in order to make use of the Ec2MultiRegionSnitch. The seed nodes that are set in the cassandra.yaml file must be the public IPs of the seed machines. Since private IPs are not routable, public IPs need to be used in order to get to the nodes that will initiate the bootstrap. The `storage_port`, default 7000 (or `ssl_storage_port`, default 7001), should be accessible to all the nodes in the cluster. This may require adjusting the security group settings. The keyspace creation with regard to data centers should be handled in the same fashion as the Ec2Snitch. Listing 5.2 shows an example of how to create a keyspace using the Ec2MultiRegionSnitch in the us-east and us-west data centers. Each data center is being set up with a replication factor of 3.

Listing 5.2 **Keyspace Creation for the Ec2MultiRegionSnitch in the us-east and us-west Data Centers**

```
CREATE KEYSPACE VideoStore
WITH replication = {'class': 'NetworkTopologyStrategy', 'us-east' : 3, 'us-west': 3 }
AND durable_writes = true;
```

Property File

As with the rest of the snitches, the PropertyFileSnitch helps to determine the location of nodes by rack and data center. The difference here is that the layout is user defined. This is good for more complex groupings that may lack uniformity (such as with the RackInferringSnitch and the EC2-based snitches). The property file for the Cassandra node sits in the same directory as the cassandra.yaml file. It is named cassandra-topology .properties.

PropertyFileSnitch Configuration

Using the PropertyFileSnitch is difficult if you have a large cluster that is not under some configuration management (such as Chef or Puppet). The cassandra-topology.properties file must be in sync on every machine in the cluster for everything to work properly. And every node in the cluster must be in this file. The typical use case for the PropertyFileSnitch is when you have nonuniform IPs in multiple data centers. The ability to specify which IPs sit in which racks and which data centers is powerful for configuring a complex setup. Listing 5.3 shows an example cassandra-topology.properties file. In this file, there are two data centers with two racks each. In both racks, the IPs are laid out in a nonuniform fashion.

Listing 5.3 **Example cassandra-topology.properties File. Setting Up Two Physical Data Centers with Two Racks Each, All with a Nonuniform Layout of IPs**

```
# Data Center One
19.82.20.3=DC1:RAC1
19.83.123.233=DC1:RAC1
19.84.193.101=DC1:RAC1
19.85.13.6=DC1:RAC1

19.23.20.87=DC1:RAC2
19.15.16.200=DC1:RAC2
19.24.102.103=DC1:RAC2
# Data Center Two
29.51.8.2=DC2:RAC1
29.50.10.21=DC2:RAC1
29.50.29.14=DC2:RAC1
53.25.29.124=DC2:RAC2
53.34.20.223=DC2:RAC2
53.14.14.209=DC2:RAC2
```

The last thing you need to ensure is that whatever you name your data centers in the cassandra-topology.properties file, the names must match the names of your data centers in the keyspace definition. The corresponding keyspace creation would have to look like Listing 5.4.

Listing 5.4 **Keyspace Creation for a PropertyFileSnitch-Based Keyspace**

```
CREATE KEYSPACE VideoStore
WITH replication = {'class': 'NetworkTopologyStrategy', 'DC1' : 2, 'DC2' : 2}
AND durable_writes = true;
```

Partitioners

The placement of replicas within a data center is determined by the partitioner. At its core, the partitioner is just a hashing function for computing the token (aka the hash) of a row key. Since the location of data within a cluster is determined by its token, it is ultimately up to the partitioner where the data ends up. Each row has its own token and is therefore uniquely identifiable. This is why each row must be able to fit in full on a single node, regardless of what the replication factor for the data center is.

Once the partitioner for a cluster has been chosen, you need to continue to use the same partitioner. Unlike compaction strategies, once the partitioner is in place, it is set for the duration of the cluster. That is not to say that you are not without options. There are a few possible partitioners you can use. As of Cassandra 1.2, you will almost always want to use the Murmur3Partitioner. Let's take a look at what options are available.

Byte Ordered

The ByteOrderedPartitioner was one of the first available in Cassandra. While it does have some advantages, it is not recommended to use this. The ByteOrderedPartitioner is used for ordered partitioning of data. This is achieved by ordering the row lexically by the key bytes. Tokens are calculated using the hex representation of the leading character in a key.

The main advantage to using an ordered partitioner is that you can do scans by primary key. This means that Cassandra will be capable of doing range scans. For example, you can say, "Show me all users in my database who have a last name between Bradberry and Lubow." The reason this type of query isn't possible with one of the random partitioners is that the token is a hashed value of the key and there is no guarantee of sequence. Even though this all seems like a great idea, you can use secondary indexes to achieve the same thing and avoid a lot of the consequences of using an ordered partitioner.

There are two major cons to using the ordered partitioner: poor load balancing and hot spots. Although it is entirely possible to get hot spots on the random partitioners as well, your chances increase with ordered partitioners. While this is application dependent, most applications tend to write sequentially or heavily favor certain types of data like timestamps or similar last names. If this is the case for your application, many of the reads and writes will go to the same few nodes and cause hot spots. These types of hot spots will also cause trouble when attempting to load-balance your data. One table being balanced across the cluster does not mean that another table will be balanced across the cluster. This means regularly recalculating and rebalancing your partition ranges. Not only is this an additional administrative headache to deal with, but it is also easily avoidable by choosing a random partitioner and being intelligent about query patterns and using secondary indexes.

Random Partitioners

A random partitioner is a partitioner that distributes data in a random but consistent fashion around the cluster. Both the RandomPartitioner and the Murmur3Partitioner are examples of random partitioners. Unlike ordered partitioners such as the ByteOrderedPartitioner, random partitioners create a hashing function that makes the distribution of data appear more random. As of Cassandra 1.2, there are two types of random partitioners: RandomPartitioner and Murmur3Partitioner.

Random

The RandomPartitioner was the default partitioner in Cassandra prior to 1.2. It should not be confused with the concept of a random partitioner. The RandomPartitioner uses an MD5 hash value of the row to evenly distribute data across the cluster. The possible range of values for the hash is from 0 to (2^{127} - 1). If you are using virtual nodes in Cassandra 1.2, you won't need to worry about calculating tokens. If you are not using vnodes, you will have to properly calculate token ranges in order to have a balanced cluster. In almost all cases, you will want to use the Murmur3Partitioner if you are using Cassandra 1.2. When using the RandomPartitioner, you can page through all rows using the `token` function in CQL 3.

Murmur3

As of Cassandra 1.2, the Murmur3Partitioner is the new default partitioner when creating a Cassandra cluster. It provides a faster hashing function called the MurmurHash. This function creates a 64-bit hash value of the row key. Its values range from -2^{63} to $(+2^{63}-1)$. The other major added benefit to using the Murmur3Partitioner is that you can page through all rows using the `token` function in CQL 3.

Node Layout

Prior to Cassandra 1.2, one token was assigned to each node. This ensured that within the ring, each node was responsible for one contiguous range of data. Virtual nodes, or vnodes, provide a Cassandra node with the ability to be responsible for many token ranges. Within the cluster, they can be noncontiguous and selected at random. This provides a greater distribution of data than the non-vnode paradigm.

Virtual Nodes

There are many advantages to using vnodes over a setup in which each node has a single token. It should be noted that you can easily have Cassandra follow the old single-token paradigm by setting `num_tokens` to 1 instead of a larger setting like 256. If you do that, you won't be able to take advantage of more efficient node bootstrapping. For example, let's say you have a 20-node cluster that has a replication factor of 3, and you lose a node and have to bring up a replacement. Without vnodes, you will be guaranteed to touch and likely saturate three nodes in your cluster (or about 15%). Since the RF is 3 and you are down one node, two replicas times three ranges (assuming that is the breakdown) means six nodes available to stream or bootstrap from. That's the theory anyway. In practice, Cassandra will use only three nodes to rebuild the data. So out of your 20-node cluster, you will have one node down for a rebuild and three nodes streaming to rebuild it. Effectively 20% of your cluster is degraded. This is all assuming nothing else happens, such as losing another node while rebuilding the current one.

Enter vnodes. Instead of only being able to stream from other nodes in the replica set that was lost, the data is spread around the cluster and can be streamed from many nodes. When it comes to repairs, the way it works is that a validation compaction is run to see what data needs to be streamed to the node being repaired. Once the validation compaction is done, the node creates a Merkle tree and sends the data from that tree to the requesting node. Of the two operations, streaming is the faster one, whereas the validation can take a long time depending on the size of the data. With smaller distributions of data, the validations on each node can be completed more quickly. Since the streaming is fast anyway, the entire process is sped up because there are more nodes handling less data and providing it to the requesting node more quickly.

Another huge advantage is the fact that replacing or adding nodes can be done individually instead of doing full capacity planning. Before virtual nodes, if you had a 12-node cluster, you could not add just one node without rebalancing. This would leave the cluster in a state where there is an uneven distribution of data. Among other things, this can create hot spots, which is bad for the cluster. With virtual nodes, you can add a single cluster and the `shuffle` method will redistribute data to ensure that everything is properly balanced throughout the cluster. If you are using older commodity machines or slightly slower machines, setting the `num_tokens` field to something smaller than the default of 256 is probably the way to go. Starting with the default of 256 is usually fine.

Balanced Clusters

If you are starting with Cassandra 1.2 or greater, you will likely be using virtual nodes, so you won't need to worry about keeping your cluster balanced. Everything related to keeping the data distribution in the cluster balanced evenly will happen in the background. You need to worry about the balance of a cluster only if you are using a partitioner where token generation isn't done for you.

Firewalls

Cassandra primarily operates using three ports: 7000 (or 7001 if you are using SSL), 7199, and 9160. In order for Cassandra to be able to properly talk to the other nodes in the ring, it should to be able to speak TCP to ports 7000 or 7001. This is the internode cluster communication port. Port 7001 is used only if internode communication is set to be encrypted. This is done by setting `internode_encryption` to either `all`, `dc`, or `rack`. The default setting of `none` will ensure that internode encryption is off and Cassandra will use port 7000 for communication.

Port 7199 is the JMX port used for the initial JMX handshake. Once the initial JMX handshake has been completed, Cassandra picks a high port, or a port greater than 1024, to continue the communication. The last and likely most important port is the Thrift client port. This is port 9160. When clients or applications connect to Cassandra, they do so on port 9160.

The other port that should typically be open in a Cassandra cluster is port 22, generally known as the SSH port. Though you can run `nodetool` queries from any Cassandra machine, you will typically want to run additional commands such as `vmstat` or `dstat`, or even look into the logs to get deeper insight into problems.

Platforms

Cassandra will run on any system that supports the Java Virtual Machine (JVM). The easiest way to get started with an actual deployment greater than your personal machine is to use a cloud service. For instance, on Amazon Web Services, there are ready-made AMIs (Amazon

Machine Images) that come preloaded with Cassandra. You can start one up and basically go right into using your Cassandra cluster. This is the reason that so much work has been done to create a snitch that is specific to Amazon's EC2 (Elastic Computer Cloud).

Amazon Web Services

If you decide to run your cluster on AWS, there are a few basic principles that should be followed. The smallest node that you should run Cassandra on is either an m1.large or an m1.xlarge with ephemeral storage. Since Amazon reduced the number of ephemeral disks per instance from four to two, you may need to attach two additional disks.

The most efficient way to make use of a basic configuration is to set up RAID0 on the ephemeral drives and put the CommitLog on that same volume. Even though it is generally considered best practice to put the CommitLog on a separate volume, using Amazon's EBS (Elastic Block Store) here would be slower, and using the root partition (which is also used by the OS itself) would cause slowdown. Therefore, sharing the RAID0 will likely yield the best results. Even though Cassandra now has JBoD support, you will likely get better throughput by using RAID0. RAID0 takes the approach of splitting every block to be on a separate device. It does this to ensure that writes are handled in parallel instead of serially.

EBS volumes on Cassandra are generally not recommended as they contend for network I/O. Adding capacity by increasing the number of EBS volumes per host also does not scale very well. It easily surpasses the ability of the system to keep effective buffer caches and concurrently serve requests for all of the data. Having very large drives on a single system also does not play well with buffer caches to be effective. Using EBS volumes is still a good idea for backups within your cluster. If you have a regular backup strategy, EBS volumes as well as Amazon S3 (and even Amazon Glacier) should be a part of it.

Other Platforms

Cassandra performs very well on any of the cloud platforms, including Rackspace, Google Compute Engine, and Windows Azure. The requirements for distribution across zones, fast consistent disk I/O, and easy base configuration layout make it well suited for any of the cloud platforms, either individually or in tandem. The value and the performance benefits of a specific cloud platform will be found by figuring out how to tune your setup best for your use case.

Summary

In this chapter, we covered the basics of how a cluster is constructed and the decisions that need to be made when creating one. These include everything from choosing the partitioner to the replication strategy. We also delved into some of the pros and cons of those issues.

Being a distributed system, Cassandra has a lot of moving parts, some that must be set prior to use and others that can be changed around even while in production. Now you should have enough information to move forward and create your cluster, knowing what kinds of trade-offs you are willing to make and where you want to get started.

6

Performance Tuning

Once your Cassandra cluster is in production and running with its out-of-the-box configuration, it's time to push the envelope a little with some performance tuning. There are multiple levels at which this tuning can take place. At the lowest level, there are the hardware and operating system. And while some of this has to do with basic setup of the hardware (such as RAID levels), there are kernel-level tunables that you can take advantage of. At the next level is the Java Virtual Machine. The JVM also has a lot of ways that it can be started and manipulated to handle various types of workloads and applications. And finally there are the configurables within Cassandra itself.

The important thing to remember when attempting to do performance tuning of any kind is that not everything is universally applicable. Your mileage will vary depending on your OS, hardware, applications, and access patterns. Learning which things are tunable and what they do when changed will go a long way toward helping you pull the most out of your system. This chapter will talk about how some of the available knobs work.

Methodology

Much of the tuning that needs to be done on any system requires a baseline understanding of how the system operates under normal circumstances. There are a number of methods that can be used to obtain this information. The most common method is to use standard *nix tools like `vmstat`, `iostat`, `dstat`, and any of the top monitors like `htop`, `atop`, and `top`. Each of these tools will give you a picture of usage on the memory, CPU, I/O, disks, and any combinations of those on your system. It may sound boring and tedious, but get a little familiar with what the output of those tools should look like under normal operating conditions for your system.

Having instrumented graphs is also helpful. Applications such as Cacti, Munin, and Ganglia come with standard templates for graphing many of the system-level metrics. This means you can actively change settings and see how the applications and the system respond in real time. While some of these may be easier than others to get working, it is easier to understand a visual representation of changes than to determine whether or not one or two numbers in a row of other numbers changed significantly. If you are using Amazon Web Services, you get a few of these graphs for free in the Web console just for having an instance running.

When making changes, you should have a control machine as well as an experimental machine. One method for testing changes is to have a query or a script run on both the control machine and the experimental machine and compare their response times. The problem with this method is that when running a query under normal circumstances, you will likely be using both of the nodes as coordinator nodes, and the response will be cached for one of the two queries by the node responsible for the data. If caching isn't on for Cassandra, you may get the file system cache. There are a number of variables here, and even though there are ways around many of them, there might be an easier (and possibly better) way to measure the effectiveness of your changes within your application or cluster.

Testing in Production

A lot of performance optimization testing can be done in production. Although making changes in a production environment goes against conventional wisdom (and might even make you feel a little uneasy), Cassandra is built to be fault tolerant. There are obviously certain circumstances when this is not possible, and even when it is, it should be done with extreme caution. If you have a three-node cluster with an RF of 1, testing performance changes in production is probably not a good idea. If you have a six-node cluster with an RF of 2 or more that is not running at capacity, you can stand to lose a node and recover if you make a mistake. If you make too big a mistake, it might even be better to pull the node out of the cluster and start from scratch by re-bootstrapping it.

On the whole, Cassandra is intended to be a resilient system. If one node goes a little funky and becomes too slow to respond, the FailureDetector will remove it without your having to do a thing. In this respect, Cassandra can protect you from yourself. The general idea is that you can take chances within reason as long as you are aware of what chances you are taking.

Tuning

Cassandra has a lot of knobs that can be twisted and turned to get different performance characteristics for different types of workloads. These settings apply to all different stages of the architecture and have varying impacts based on the types of workloads you are seeing.

Timeouts

There are quite a few configurable timeouts in Cassandra. The proper values for these settings are highly dependent on your environment and your system requirements. They include how long the coordinator node in a query should wait for operations to return. Setting the proper timeouts for your environment is critical. If you set the values too high, your queries will start to stack up while coordinator nodes wait for responses from slow or down nodes. If the settings are too low, coordinator nodes will give responses based on incomplete information and the replica sets will have been queried for data that wasn't returned to the application.

Another configurable value is `streaming_socket_timeout_in_ms`. This is an important setting as it can control how much time is spent restreaming data between nodes in the event of a timeout. By default, there is no timeout in Cassandra for streaming operations. It is a good idea to set a timeout, but not too low a timeout. If a streaming operation times out, the file being streamed is started over from the beginning. As some SSTables can have a not insignificant amount of data, ensure that the value is set high enough to avoid unnecessary streaming restarts.

Cassandra provides a setting that allows nodes to communicate timeout information to each other. This option is called `cross_node_timeout` and defaults to `false`. The reason this is initially off is because the timing can properly be synchronized only if system clocks on all nodes are in sync. This is usually accomplished with an NTP (Network Time Protocol) server. If this setting is disabled, Cassandra assumes that the request was instantly forwarded by a coordinator node to the replica.

CommitLog

The idea of a CommitLog and how Cassandra has implemented it is one of the reasons that Cassandra responds so well to write-heavy workloads. Here are some tricks for optimizing the CommitLog.

An easy optimization for Cassandra is putting your CommitLog directory on a separate drive from your data directories. CommitLog segments are written to every time a MemTable is flushed to disk. This might be easier said than done depending on your setup. If your servers are hosted in AWS, the instance stores are your best bet for CommitLog segments on standard machines. On the hi1.large instances in AWS, which allow you to use solid-state drives (SSDs), you have access to multiple faster devices than just the ephemeral drives. But the idea is that you can search the CommitLog and the data SSTables simultaneously, giving better read and write performance. It may not be as easy to add a drive to a Cassandra server running on iron. It would include downtime for the machine, which is not a problem for Cassandra assuming that your downtime period is less than your setting for `max_window_in_ms`.

In the cassandra.yaml file, there is a setting called `commitlog_directory`. That setting is the one that determines where the CommitLog segments get written to. Check to see which disk or partition your `data_directory` is set to in the cassandra.yaml file and make sure the directory of the CommitLog is set to be on a different disk or partition. By ensuring that the `data_directory` and `commitlog_directory` are on different partitions, the CommitLog reads/writes don't affect the overall performance of the rest of the reads on the node.

There are also a few other settings in the cassandra.yaml file that affect the performance of the CommitLog. The `commitlog_sync` setting can be set to either `batch` or `sync`. If the `commitlog_sync` is set to `batch`, Cassandra will block until the write has been synced to disk. Having the `commitlog_sync` set to `batch` is usually not needed, as under most circumstances writes aren't acknowledged until another node has the data. On the other hand, `periodic` is the default setting and typically is the best for performance as well. You will also need to ensure that the `commitlog_sync_period_in_ms` is sensible for your write workload. For durability, if you have a high-volume write system, set this to something smaller than 10,000ms (or 10s) to ensure minimal data loss between flushes.

Although the default setting of 32 for `commitlog_segment_size_in_mb` is a sane default, depending on your backup strategy, this may be something you want to change. If you are doing CommitLog archiving as a form of backup, choosing a more granular setting of 8 or 16 might be better. This allows a finer point-in-time restore, depending on what your volume is.

MemTables

There are a few basic tenets to keep in mind when adjusting MemTable thresholds:

- Larger MemTables take memory away from caches. Since MemTables store the actual column data, they will take up at least that amount of space plus a little extra for index structure overhead. Therefore, your settings should take into account schema (ColumnFamily and column layout) in addition to overall memory.
- Larger MemTables do not improve write performance. This is because writes are happening to memory anyway. There is no way to speed up this process unless your CommitLog and SSTables are on separate volumes. If the CommitLog and SSTables were to share a volume, they would be in contention for I/O.
- Larger MemTables are better for unbatched writes. If you do batch writing, you will likely not see a large benefit. But if you do unbatched writes, the compaction will have a better effect on the read performance as it will do a better job of grouping like data together.
- Larger MemTables lead to more effective compaction. Having a lot of little MemTables is bad as it leads to a lot of turnover. It also leads to a lot of additional seeks when the read requests hit memory.

The performance tuning of MemTables can double as a pressure release valve if your Cassandra nodes start to get overloaded. They shouldn't be your only method of emergency release, but they can act as a good complement. In the cassandra.yaml file, there is a setting called `flush_largest_memtables_at`. The default setting is 0.75. This setting is a percentage. What is going on under the hood is that every time a full garbage collection (GC) is completed, the heap usage is checked. If the amount of memory used is still greater than (the default) 0.75, the largest MemTables will be flushed. This setting is more effective when used under read-heavy workloads. In write-heavy workloads, there will probably be too little memory freed too late in the cycle to be of significant value. If you notice the heap filling up from MemTables frequently, you may need to either add more capacity or adjust the heap setting in the JVM.

The `memtable_total_space_in_mb` setting in the cassandra.yaml is usually commented out by default. When it is commented out, Cassandra will automatically set the value to one-third the size of the heap. You typically don't need to adjust this setting as one-third of the heap is sufficient. If you are in a write-heavy environment, you may want to increase this value. Since you already know the size of the JVM heap, you can just calculate what the new size of the total space allotted for MemTables should be. Try not to be too aggressive here as stealing memory from other parts of Cassandra can have negative consequences.

The setting of `memtable_flush_writers` is another one that comes unset out of the box. By default, it's set to the number of data directories defined in the cassandra.yaml. If you have a large heap size and your use case is having Cassandra under a write-heavy workload, this value can be safely increased.

On a similar note, the `memtable_flush_queue_size` has an effect on the speed and efficiency of a MemTable flush. This value determines the number of MemTables to allow to wait for a writer thread to flush to disk. This should be set, at a minimum, to the maximum number of secondary indexes created on a single ColumnFamily. In other words, if you have a ColumnFamily with ten secondary indexes, this value should be 10. The reason for this is that if the `memtable_flush_queue_size` is set to 2 and you have three secondary indexes on a ColumnFamily, there are two options available: either flush the MemTable and each index not updated during the initial flush will be out of sync with the SSTable data, or the new SSTable won't be loaded into memory until all the indexes have been updated. To avoid either of these scenarios, it is recommended that the value of `mem_table_flush_queue_size` be set to ensure that all secondary indexes for a ColumnFamily can be updated at flush time.

Concurrency

Cassandra was designed to have faster write performance than read performance. One of the ways this is achieved is using threads for concurrency. There are two settings in the cassandra.yaml that allow control over the amount of concurrency: `concurrent_reads` and `concurrent_writes`. By default, both of these values are set to 32. Since the writes that come to Cassandra go to memory, the bottleneck for most performance is going to the disk for reads. To calculate the best setting for `concurrent_reads`, the value should be 16 * $number_of_drives. If you have two drives, you can leave the default value of 32. The reason for this is to ensure that the operating system has enough room to decide which reads should be serviced at what time.

Coming back to writes, since they go directly to memory, the work is CPU bound as opposed to being I/O bound like reads. To derive the best setting for `concurrent_writes`, you should use 8 * number_of_cores in your system. If you have a quad-core dual-processor system, the total number of cores is eight and the `concurrent_writes` should be set at 64.

Durability and Consistency

Something to always keep in mind when looking at the performance of your application is which trade-offs you are willing to make with regard to the durability of your data on write and the consistency of your data on read. Much of this can be achieved by setting consistency levels on reads and writes. For reference, a quorum is calculated (rounded down to a whole number) as (replication_factor/2) + 1.

We have already covered consistency levels in detail, but the theory behind when to use which consistency level at what time, known as durability, is also important. When you are working under a write-heavy workload, it is unlikely that all the data being written is so important that it needs to be verified as received by every node in a replica (`QUORUM`, `LOCAL_QUORUM`, `EACH_QUORUM`, or `ALL`). Unless your node or cluster is under a heavy load, you will probably be safe with using `CL.ANY` or `CL.ONE` for most writes. This reduces the amount of network traffic and reduces the wait time on the application performing the write (which is typically a blocking operation to begin with). If you can decide at write time or connection time which data is important enough to require higher consistency levels in your writes, you can save quite a bit of round-trip and wait time on your write calls.

On the read side of things, you can ask yourself a similar question: How important is the accuracy of the call I am making? Since you are working under eventual consistency, it is important to remember that the latest and greatest version of the data may not always be immediately available on every node. If you are running queries that require the latest version of the data, you may want to run the query with `QUORUM`, `LOCAL_QUORUM`, `EACH_QUORUM`, or `ALL`. It is important to note when using `ALL` that the read will fail if one of the replicas does not respond to the coordinator. If it is acceptable for the data not to have the latest timestamp, using `CL.ONE` may be a good option. By default, a read repair will run in the background to ensure that for whatever query you just ran, all data is consistent.

If latency is an issue, you should also consider using `CL.ONE`. If consistency is more important to you, you can ensure that a read will always reflect the most recent write by using the following: (nodes_written + nodes_read) > replication_factor.

When thinking about consistency levels in the context of multiple data centers, it is important to remember the additional latency incurred by needing to wait for a response from the remote data center or data centers. Ideally, you want all of an application's requests to be served from within the same data center, which will help avoid quite a bit of latency. It is important to keep in mind that even at a consistency level of `ONE` or `LOCAL_QUORUM`, a write is still sent to all replicas, including those in other data centers. In this case, the consistency level determines how many replicas are required to respond that they received the write.

Compression

There are a few options for using compression and taking advantage of what it has to offer. There is compression at the file system level, compression at the ColumnFamily level, and compression at the network level.

Network compression is available for dealing with internode communication. In the cassandra.yaml file, the option `internode_compression` controls whether traffic moving between Cassandra nodes should be compressed. There are a few options here. You can choose to ignore compression completely, compress all traffic, or only compress traffic between different data centers. It is likely that this setting will not have a major effect on your system any way you set it. The default is to compress all traffic, and this is a sane default. Compression is CPU bound. If you are short on CPU resources (and it's rare that

Cassandra is CPU bound), not compressing any traffic will likely net a performance bonus. You can also incrementally save here by just setting it to only compress between data centers (assuming you have more than one data center).

Prior to Cassandra 1.1.0, compression at the ColumnFamily level was turned off by default. The option to use either SnappyCompressor or DeflateCompressor has been around since Cassandra 1.0.0. Cassandra post-1.1.0 has the Java Snappy compression library as the default compression for a ColumnFamily. Out of the box, you can get a pretty good speed increase by just enabling some compression algorithm across all of the ColumnFamilys. In addition to saving space on disk, compression also reduces actual disk I/O. This is especially true for read-heavy workloads. Since the data on disk is compressed, Cassandra only needs to find the location of the rows in the SSTable index and decompress the relevant row chunks. All this ultimately means that larger data sets can now fit into memory, which means quicker access times. The speed increase on writes happens because the data is compressed when the MemTable is flushed to disk. This results in a lot less I/O. As a negative, it adds a little more CPU overhead to the flush. Typically, this is negligible compared to the performance gains. With all these factors considered together, using compression is highly recommended.

With either SnappyCompressor or DeflateCompressor, you have the additional option of setting `chunk_length_kb`. This tells the compression library what the compression chunk size in kilobytes should be. The default value is 64KB. This is a fairly sane default and should probably be left alone unless you know the makeup of the ColumnFamily prior to creating it. With wide row ColumnFamilys, 64KB allows reading slices of column data without decompressing the entire row. On the skinny row side, it is slightly less efficient as you may end up decompressing more data than you want. If you approximate the layout of your rows, you can adjust the value accordingly. To determine a good `chunk_length_kb` value, you will need to determine how much data is typically requested at a time and figure out how that fits into the average size of a row in the ColumnFamily (which can be found using `nodetool cfstats`). You can also adjust the `crc_check_chance`. There is a cyclic redundancy check (CRC) checksum attached to every compressed block. By default, it is checked every read. You can disable this by setting the value to 0, but it is not recommended to do this. A better approach would be a setting of 0.5 to check the checksum every other read instead of every read.

If you have an existing ColumnFamily for which you are changing the compression settings, the already-created SSTables on disk are not compressed immediately. Any new SSTable that gets created will be compressed. You can then either let the existing SSTables get compressed during normal compactions or force the SSTables to be rebuilt by using `nodetool scrub`. Both are acceptable options and can easily be done in conjunction in larger clusters.

It is possible to use another compression option or even to implement your own. All that is necessary is to implement a compression class using the org.apache.cassandra.io .compress.ICompressor interface. While there may be good reason to implement your own compression class, the defaults that ship with Cassandra are good for the majority of use cases.

SnappyCompressor

Snappy is a compression/decompression library tailored to the 64-bit CPU architecture and aims to be high speed with reasonable compression size. As a barometer, it usually compresses things within the same range as LZF. Since Cassandra is written in Java, it uses the Java port of the original library written in C++. If you have a read-heavy workload, you will want to stick with SnappyCompressor.

DeflateCompressor

The DeflateCompressor, more commonly known as Java's version of zip, is more often used when you want better compression ratios. Your reads might come a little slower, but your data on disk will be smaller than if you were using SnappyCompressor.

File System

There are a number of options for which file system to use. If you are interested in getting better use of your disk while still keeping some speed, it might be worthwhile to look into using ZFS. The common deployment file system for Linux is ext4 and is already supported by most modern Linux distributions. Formatting a device for ext4 is straightforward (see Listing 6.1), and the utility for doing so is available out of the box.

Listing 6.1 **Format a Drive with the ext4 File System**

```
$ mke2fs -t ext4 /dev/md0
```

By default, ext4 is a fairly performant file system. By changing a few settings (also known as mount options) in the /etc/fstab, you can get a little extra performance push.

- **`noatime.`** This stands for "no access time" updates. It tells the operating system not to update the inode information on each access. This is useful because Cassandra doesn't access inode information and there is no need to pay the performance penalty for updating it.
- **`barriers=0.`** This option, when set to 0, disables write barriers. Write barriers enforce the proper on-disk order of journal commits. Since ext4 is a journal-based file system, you incur a performance penalty when ensuring the order of the journals. With hardware-based systems, it is safe to disable barriers if you have battery-backed disks (as is common to hardware RAIDs).
- **`data=journal, commit=15.`** By default, the operating system will sync all data (including metadata) to disk every five seconds. By extending this value, you can improve performance. `commit` applies only if you set `data=journal`.
- **`data=writeback, nobh.`** When you set `data=writeback`, metadata for files is lazily written after the file is written. While this won't cause file system corruption, it may cause the most recent changes to be lost in the event of a crash. Since most files in Cassandra are written on and not edited in place, this is a low-risk change. `nobh` (no buffer heads) refers to the operating system's attempt to avoid associating buffer

heads to data pages. In other words, don't create a map of the disk block information. This is a useful setting for Cassandra because it doesn't update in place.

Note that if you make changes on a disk that is already mounted, you will have to unmount and remount the disk in order for the changes to take effect.

Caching

The use of caching is an important part of getting performance out of any system. Caching is the ability to store something in a temporary location that makes it faster or easier to access than getting it the way it would otherwise be retrieved. In other words, you don't go to the store to buy a glass of milk. You buy a gallon of milk, store it in your fridge, and then go to your fridge when you want a glass of milk.

Cache works the same way. Assuming that you have row caching on, if you are constantly going back to get the same row from a ColumnFamily and that row isn't located on the coordinator node, the coordinator node and the queried node will cache it. The next time the coordinator is asked for that row, it will go to the temporary store (cache) and check that location first. If it finds the data in the cache, this will negate the need to check the node actually responsible for the data. This means there will be less disk I/O, less network traffic, and less system overhead that doesn't need to be dedicated to listening for query results externally.

How Cassandra Caching Works

Before we talk specifically about tuning the cache, we should discuss how caching in Cassandra works. When both the row cache and key cache are configured and enabled, the standard order for searching for the data is row cache, key cache, SSTables, and then MemTables. Let's break this down a little bit further.

When your application requests a row of data, the first thing that Cassandra does is to go to the row cache. If Cassandra finds the row in the row cache, it returns it to the application and that is a win for caching. If the row is not cached, Cassandra checks the SSTables on disk. If the row isn't in the SSTables, the MemTables are checked. Wherever the row was found, whether in the SSTables or the MemTables, the row cache will be populated with the value returned for that row. If the application requests a column and the row where that column resides is already in the row cache, Cassandra will grab the row from the cache, pull the column out, and return it to the application.

General Caching Tips

Here are some general rules that you can follow to get efficient use of caching:

- Store less recently used data or wide rows in a ColumnFamily with minimal or no caching.
- Try to create logical separations of heavily read data. This can be done by breaking your frequently used data apart into many ColumnFamilys and tuning the caching on each ColumnFamily individually.

- Add more Cassandra nodes. Since Cassandra does a lot of caching for you, you will get a pretty solid benefit from adding nodes. Each node will then contain a smaller data set, and you will be able to fit more data in memory.

The other item to be aware of when it comes to caching is how it affects the MemTables. A Cassandra MemTable requires an index structure in addition to the data that it stores. This is so that the MemTable is easily searchable for data that has not been written to an SSTable yet. If the size of the values stored is small compared to the number of rows and columns in that MemTable, the overhead to support this indexing may not be worth it.

Global Cache Tuning

There is an easy performance gain to be had if you have a small data set per node. The first thing we need to do is define *small* in this scenario. Small refers to the data set being able to fit into memory. In the cassandra.yaml file, the setting `populate_io_cache_on_flush` is set to `false` by default. This is because it is expected that most data sets will not be able to fit into memory. If yours does, it means the cache will be populated on MemTable flush and compactions. This will greatly speed up your query times by having all data loaded into the cache immediately when it becomes available.

One of the most common types of caches for a database is a key cache. Cassandra gives you the ability to control the maximum size of the key cache. By default, the `key_cache_size_in_mb` is set to 5% of the heap in megabytes or 100MB, whichever is less. The key cache saves one seek each hit. And although the default value is relatively sane, it probably makes sense to increase the size. The actual value that you set it to depends on how much memory you have.

The amount of time that the keys are saved in the key cache is four hours by default. As with many of the other settings, changing it depends on your use case. Four hours is a decent default, but if you have daily data, perhaps changing it to 24 hours would make more sense in the context of your application.

Similar options are available for tuning the row cache. The row cache, when a cache hit happens, saves at least two seeks, sometimes more. Since it is easy for the row cache to become really large, really quick, it needs to be adjusted for your use case. You need to ensure that you set a `row_cache_size_in_mb` that makes sense for the average size of your rows relative to your heap size. As with keys, you also have the ability to set the `row_cache_save_period`. This value comes disabled by default, meaning that the rows aren't saved to disk. Saving caches to disk greatly increases Cassandra cold-start speeds and has relatively little impact on I/O. But in general, saving the row cache to disk is much more expensive than saving the key cache to disk and has a fairly limited use.

There is also the ability to change the provider being used for the row cache. As of Cassandra 1.2, there are two possibilities, ConcurrentLinkedHashCacheProvider and SerializingCacheProvider. The SerializingCacheProvider serializes the contents of the row and stores them off the JVM heap. Serialized rows use less memory than a full row inside the JVM, giving you the ability to store more information in a smaller memory footprint.

Storing the cache off-heap also means smaller heap sizes, reducing the impact of GC pauses. The ConcurrentLinkedHashCacheProvider is better for workloads that are update heavy. This is because ConcurrentLinkedHashCacheProvider updates data in place. The SerializingCacheProvider invalidates the cached row only on update, meaning that the seek still has to go to disk to get the correct data. Technically, there is a third option for a row cache. It would be to build a custom cache provider. As long as the provider implements org.apache.cassandra.cache.IRowCacheProvider, it can be used as a caching engine. However, the default available options are fine for most use cases.

ColumnFamily Cache Tuning

There are four possible settings for caching within a ColumnFamily: `ALL`, `NONE`, `KEYS_ONLY`, and `ROWS_ONLY`. They all do exactly what they sound as if they do. `NONE` is to disable caching on the ColumnFamily. `KEYS_ONLY` is to cache only by keys requested. `ROWS_ONLY` is to cache the entire row of a requested key. `ALL` refers to the ability to cache as much information as possible. The option that you choose should be relevant to the workload that you normally put on Cassandra.

A good way to think about this is to look at your query pattern. If you have skinny rows and you are asking Cassandra for the same row over and over, using `ROWS_ONLY` is likely the route for you. It allows the row to be put into the cache and modified only if the row itself is modified. If you have wide rows and you don't use most of the keys in the row, it might make more sense to use `KEYS_ONLY` as the cache. Using `KEYS_ONLY` makes sense only if you don't have a lot of turnover in the cache. If you do have a lot of turnover, it may make sense not to do any caching at all. This means setting the cache to `NONE`. Listing 6.2 shows how to change the cache setting on the events table to `KEYS_ONLY` using CQL 3.

Listing 6.2 **Change the Cache Setting on an Existing Table**

```
# ALTER TABLE events WITH caching='KEYS_ONLY';
```

Bloom Filters

Bloom filters are a space-efficient probabilistic data structure that allows you to test whether or not an element is a member of a set. Bloom filters allow for false positives, but not for false negatives. Cassandra uses these data structures to determine whether or not an SSTable has data for a particular row. They are used only in index queries, not in range queries.

Since by definition bloom filters allow you to customize the level of accuracy of your data structure, Cassandra passes that ability along to you. If you set the `bloom_filter_fp_chance` high, the bloom filter will use less memory but will require more disk I/O. You can disable bloom filters completely if you set the `bloom_filter_fp_chance` to 1.0.

The right bloom filter setting depends on your workload. If you have an analytics cluster that does mostly range scanning, having bloom filters would not be necessary.

Also, using LeveledCompaction typically causes slightly less fragmentation within the SSTable than SizeTieredCompaction. Therefore, the default value of the `bloom_filter_fp_chance` can be slightly higher. Keep in mind that memory savings are nonlinear. That means that going from a setting of 0.01 to 0.1 saves one-third of the memory even though you are changing the `bloom_filter_fp_chance` by an order of magnitude.

In Cassandra version 1.2, bloom filters are stored off-heap. This means that you don't need to think about the size of the bloom filters when attempting to figure out the maximum memory size for the JVM. You can easily alter the `bloom_filter_fp_chance` setting on a per-ColumnFamily basis, as shown in Listing 6.3.

Listing 6.3 **Adjust the Bloom Filter False Positive Chance for an Existing ColumnFamily**

```
# ALTER TABLE events WITH bloom_filter_fp_chance = 0.01;
```

Once you update the `bloom_filter_fp_chance` for a ColumnFamily, you need to regenerate the bloom filters. This can be done either by forcing a compaction or by running `upgradesstables` through `nodetool`.

Another good way to see if your bloom filter settings can be adjusted is through a little bit of trial and error. If you do a `nodetool cfstats`, you will be able to see the number of bloom filter false positives and the bloom filter false positive ratio for a specific ColumnFamily. You want to minimize the number of bloom filter false positives you get in general. But you also have a little leeway when adjusting the `bloom_filter_fp_chance` before you actually start getting a significant number of false positives. You will have to tune the value to see where your false positive rate starts to increase.

System Tuning

Out of the box, Linux comes configured to run pretty well. Since running Cassandra is not a normal workload for the basic server configuration, you can make a few small tweaks and get a noticeable performance improvement.

Testing I/O Concurrency

A great way to tune for reads and writes at the same time is to run a quick test with `iostat` (*nix only). In a terminal window, start `iostat` running with extended disk information and have it refresh roughly every three seconds: `iostat -x 3`. Now open up two other terminal windows. In one of those windows, start a long write process using the `dd` command (see Listing 6.4).

Listing 6.4 **Use `dd` to Measure Sequential Write Performance**

```
dd if=/dev/urandom of=/data/cassandra/test_outfile count=512 bs=1024k
```

In the other terminal window, start a long sequential read process (see Listing 6.5).

Listing 6.5 **Use `dd` to Measure Sequential Read Performance**

```
dd if=/data/cassandra/test_outfile of=/dev/null bs=4096k
```

Now look back at the `iostat` output, which is still continuing to run on the first terminal window that you opened. Did either the read or write time drop significantly? If the answer is yes, you may want to think about better separation. If you have already decided to separate the CommitLog data directory and the data directories onto different disks, you are on the right track.

Extending this idea a little further, building a more performant Cassandra node from the I/O perspective can easily be accomplished with some planning. It is common to put Cassandra data directories on a RAID drive. This isn't a bad idea as RAID provides redundancy and a little bit of extra speed, depending on which RAID level you use. But Cassandra offers a feature called JBoD (just a bunch of disks).

This example is a little contrived, as it is not indicative of regular system performance. The idea here is just to get a feel for what happens to response times when the disks are under load. It also gives you the ability to tune your current setup when there is an existing simultaneous read and write load. Again, even though the reads and writes as a result of the queries aren't normally sequential, they will likely be concurrent. This usage of `dd` mimics the concurrency aspect of the load.

Virtual Memory and Swap

If you are running Cassandra on a dedicated machine, the suggested swap setting is to keep it off. The ideal case in a bad scenario with regard to memory is that the OS kills off the Java process running Cassandra, leaving the OS reachable even if Cassandra is down. If the machine is allowed to swap itself "to death," you will have no way to get to the machine to fix it.

The settings in Linux that control these are `swappiness`, `overcommit_memory`, and `overcommit_ratio`. In the preceding scenario, `overcommit_memory` should be set to 2 and `swappiness` should be set to 0. An `overcommit_memory` setting of 2 will ensure that Linux will not hand out anonymous pages of memory unless it is sure it has a place to store them in physical memory (RAM). A `swappiness` setting of 0 tells the kernel to avoid swapping processes out of physical memory for as long as possible.

By default, Linux attempts to be smart and limits the maximum number of memory map areas that a process may have. Most applications don't need many maps. Since Cassandra works a lot with memory, it is a good idea to give it a little bit of headroom. The default for this setting is 65,535 maps. While this is fine most of the time, setting it to something higher is a good idea. A safe value for a high-volume machine and one that is commonly used on Cassandra nodes is 262,140, or four times the default setting.

sysctl Network Settings

There are a few other sysctl settings that can be adjusted for getting more performance out of your Cassandra machine. They are relevant to the amount of network traffic that is allowed in and out of the node. Listing 6.6 shows changes to the send and receive buffer sizes to tell the Linux kernel to allow for higher throughput of network traffic.

Listing 6.6 **sysctl Settings to Allow for Higher Throughput of Network Traffic**

```
net.core.rmem_max = 16777216
net.core.wmem_max = 16777216
net.ipv4.tcp_rmem = 4096 65536 16777216
net.ipv4.tcp_wmem = 4096 65536 16777216
```

File Limit Settings

You will also need to ensure that Cassandra isn't being limited by the number of files allowed by the kernel. This can be done by giving a larger value to fs.file-max in your sysctl settings. A good setting for this is 1,048,576.

In addition to changing the sysctl setting, you will need to raise the open file limit for the system. By adding the two lines in Listing 6.7 to your /etc/security/limits.conf, you should be able to give Cassandra enough room to operate under normal and heavy loads.

Listing 6.7 **/etc/security/limits.conf Settings for Allowing Additional Open Files**

```
* soft   nofile   16,384
* hard   nofile   32,768
```

Solid-State Drives

Although Cassandra's storage engine was optimized for spinning disks, you can still benefit a lot from the use of SSDs. This is evident because most modern SATA drives are best at sequential operations. Seek times are limited by the time it takes the drive to rotate. As good throughput as SATA drives get (a 7,200rpm drive typically gets around 125MB/s), solid-state drives are just better at it. They usually get about 250MB/s read and 205MB/s write throughput.

Since Cassandra writes sequentially and uses streaming write patterns, it minimizes the effects of write amplification associated with SSDs. Write amplification is a concept associated with solid-state drives where the amount of physical information written is a multiple of the logical amount intended to be written. This means that Cassandra does a good job of giving normal consumer-level SSDs a longer life span.

If you are running on hardware (or even in the cloud) and are lucky enough to have Cassandra on solid-state drives, there are a few settings you can change to get even better performance. The first change that you will want to make is to set multithreaded_compaction to true. The reason this value defaults to false is that compactions are usually I/O bound. With multithreaded compaction enabled, every compaction operation will use up to one thread per core plus one thread per SSTable being merged. This means a lot of extra disk access. If you are running on SSDs, this additional I/O won't be a problem and your bottleneck for compactions will likely become the CPU.

The other Cassandra options for tuning SSDs are `trickle_fsync` and `trickle_fsync_interval_in_kb`. These values control the intervals at which fsyncs to disk happen. When doing sequential writes to SSDs, you want to avoid sudden dirty buffer flushing from impacting read latencies. Setting `trickle_fsync` to `true` and giving a small interval (10MB is usually a good starting point) should make the dirty buffer flushes forced by the OS less frequent.

JVM Tuning

There are a lot of options for tuning the Java Virtual Machine. The best changes are going to be a result of your workload. There are a lot of "your mileage may vary"-type suggestions. In the following sections, we discuss a few basic principles that can be followed.

Multiple JVM Options

There are a few different JVMs available. The requirements for deciding which JVM to use for Cassandra are pretty straightforward. It must, at a minimum, be Java 1.6 compatible or greater. It should support whichever hardware and operating system's you are using in your infrastructure as well. Although it should run on the IBM JVM and JRockit, the recommended JVM is the Oracle/Sun JVM. Different JVMs will give you different performance characteristics, and you will have to experiment with which virtual machine is best for you and your environment.

Maximum Heap Size

The first thing that administrators usually toy with when tuning JVM settings is the maximum heap size. The option for this is `-Xmx$size`, where `$size` is the desired maximum size of the JVM heap. This value is set in your conf/cassandra-env.sh file and is defined as `MAX_HEAP_SIZE`. A good place to start is figuring out how much memory you have on the machine and cutting it in half. You will definitely need to leave enough memory for the operating system to be able to function properly. The operating system is fairly intelligent about its memory management, so it is usually smarter to slightly underallocate to the JVM. To determine the approximate size of Cassandra's internal data structures, a good rule of thumb is memtable_throughput_in_mb * 3 * number_of_hot_CFs + 1G + internal_caches.

Another important option in tuning the JVM is to set the thread stack size, `-Xss$size`. In Java, each thread has its own stack that holds function call or method arguments, return addresses, and the like. In other words, by setting the `-Xss` parameter, you are able to limit the amount of memory consumed by an individual thread. Setting this to 128KB is typically a safe bet. You should consider raising this value only if you see `OutOfMemoryError` errors with the additional message that Java is unable to create new native threads. Even then, most of the time it will be indicative of another problem that should be handled first.

If you find yourself needing to set a larger heap size and you are beginning to run short on memory (and you are using the Oracle JVM), you can look at allowing the JVM to compress ordinary object pointers. An ordinary object pointer (OOP) is a managed pointer to an object in the JVM. Normally, an object pointer in Java is the same size as the machine pointer. When CPU architectures switched to 64-bit, the size of the pointers in the JVM heap increased with it. By adding the option to compress pointers, you can reduce their impact on the heap. You can do this by adding the value `-XX:+UseCompressedOops` to your conf/cassandra-env.sh file.

Garbage Collection

Many issues that stem from JVM performance can usually be traced back to garbage collection. Periodic garbage collections usually are not a problem as most applications expect them and are fairly tolerant of them. Adjusting a few GC-related settings should help to minimize the JVM pauses that can be a result of rapid allocation and deallocation of memory inside the JVM. The following options should be set in the cassandra-env.sh as well:

- **`-XX:+UserParNewGC.`** ParNew is a "stop the world while I collect the garbage" system. This may seem like a bad idea, but this GC usually runs quickly and is responsible only for cleaning up the "younger" generation.
- **`-XX:+UseConcMarkSweepGC.`** This setting tells the JVM to allow the concurrent collector to run with the parallel young generation collector (also known as `ParNewGC` in this case).
- **`-XX: +CMSParallelRemarkEnabled.`** `CMS` here stands for `ConcurrentMarkSweep` (referenced above). This setting tells the JVM that when the CMS GC is running, the garbage collector can use multiple threads. This usually decreases the length of a pause during the phase.
- **`-XX: CMSInitiatingOccupancyFraction=75.`** If this value is not set at runtime, the JVM will attempt to determine a good value. This is a percentage and refers to the percent occupancy of the tenured generation at which a CMS GC is triggered.
- **`-XX:+UseCMSInitiatingOccupancyOnly.`** This value just tells the JVM not to try to calculate its own value for `CMSInitiatingOccupancyFraction` and to use the one provided to it.

While these settings are good generally applicable settings for Cassandra, they are mostly for systems with smaller amounts of memory, roughly 20GB or less. With anything larger, you will start to see diminishing returns on changes you make. Java will be forced to take a much larger part in memory management and garbage collection. This will invariably take up more CPU time and cause longer pauses. A common solution is to run multiple instances of Cassandra on the same node, ensuring that the token ranges don't coincide with the same replica.

Summary

As with any performance optimizations, your mileage may vary. We have covered suggestions for how to get performance improvements up and down the stack from the hardware layer all the way up to the Cassandra application and a few things in between. As is common to most bits of advice, you'll have to test things out and see what works for you. There are many additional options for tuning the Java Virtual Machine for your workload.

Determining a specific configuration or set of configuration parameters that works for you will make a large difference in the long run. It's also a good idea to always keep an eye out for best practices and to learn from people who run similar configurations or have similar requirements. There isn't always one right answer, and getting the most out of your Cassandra cluster will require some testing. Start applying some of the ideas discussed in this chapter to your cluster piecemeal and watch for improvements. Always ensure that you have a proper baseline of performance before making a change. The more you learn about how your cluster performs under load, the more you will be able to optimize its performance.

7

Maintenance

At this point, your cluster is up and running. There is data coming in and everything seems to be humming along. But Cassandra is not a set-it-and-forget-it system. Maintenance is required, and there are tools to help you perform the necessary maintenance tasks.

Understanding `nodetool`

The most basic command that you should be familiar with when administering a Cassandra cluster is `nodetool`. `nodetool` is a command-line interface to Cassandra cluster management. It can provide you with basic information about an individual node or all nodes in the cluster or ring.

As of Cassandra 1.2, `nodetool` provides the options shown in Listing 7.1.

Listing 7.1 `nodetool` **Output**

```
usage: java org.apache.cassandra.tools.NodeCmd --host <arg> <command>

-a,--include-all-sstables     includes sstables that are already on the
                              most recent version during upgradesstables.
-cf,--column-family <arg>     only take a snapshot of the specified column family.
-et,--end-token <arg>         token at which repair range ends.
-h,--host <arg>               node hostname or ip address.
-local,--in-local-dc          only repair against nodes in the same datacenter.
-p,--port <arg>               remote jmx agent port number.
-pr,--partitioner-range       only repair the first range returned by the
                              partitioner for the node.
-pw,--password <arg>          remote jmx agent password.
-snapshot,--with-snapshot     repair one node at a time using snapshots.
-st,--start-token <arg>       token at which repair range starts.
-T,--tokens                   display all tokens.
-t,--tag <arg>                optional name to give a snapshot.
-u,--username <arg>           remote jmx agent username.
```

(Continues)

Listing 7.1 nodetool **Output *(continued)***

```
Available commands
  ring                         - Print information about the token ring.
  join                         - Join the ring.
  info [-T/--tokens]           - Print node information (uptime, load, ...).
  status                       - Print cluster information (state, load, IDs, ...).
  cfstats                      - Print statistics on column families.
  version                      - Print cassandra version.
  tpstats                      - Print usage statistics of thread pools.
  proxyhistograms              - Print statistic histograms for network operations.
  drain                        - Drain the node (stop accepting writes and flush
                                 all column families).
  decommission                 - Decommission the *node I am connecting to*.
  compactionstats              - Print statistics on compactions.
  disablebinary                - Disable native transport (binary protocol).
  enablebinary                 - Reenable native transport (binary protocol).
  statusbinary                 - Status of native transport (binary protocol).
  disablehandoff               - Disable the future hints storing on the current node.
  enablehandoff                - Reenable the future hints storing on the current
                                 node.
  resumehandoff                - Resume hints delivery process.
  pausehandoff                 - Pause hints delivery process.
  disablegossip                - Disable gossip (effectively marking the node down).
  enablegossip                 - Reenable gossip.
  disablethrift                - Disable thrift server.
  enablethrift                 - Reenable thrift server.
  enablebackup                 - Enable incremental backup.
  disablebackup                - Disable incremental backup.
  statusthrift                 - Status of thrift server.
  gossipinfo                   - Shows the gossip information for the cluster.
  invalidatekeycache           - Invalidate the key cache.
  invalidaterowcache           - Invalidate the row cache.
  resetlocalschema             - Reset node's local schema and resync.
  netstats [host]              - Print network information on provided host
                                 connecting node by default).
  move <new token>             - Move node on the token ring to a new token. (for
                                 -ve tokens, use \\ to escape, Example: move
                                 \\-123).
  removenode status|force|<ID>- Show status of current node removal, force comp-
                                 letion of pending removal or remove provided ID.
  setcompactionthroughput      - Set the MB/s throughput cap for compaction in the
 <value_in_mb>                   system, or 0 to disable throttling.
  setstreamthroughput          - Set the MB/s throughput cap for streaming in the
 <value_in_mb>                   system, or 0 to disable throttling.
  describering [keyspace]      - Shows the token ranges info of a given keyspace.
  rangekeysample               - Shows the sampled keys held across all keyspaces.
  rebuild [src-dc-name]        - Rebuild data by streaming from other nodes
                                 (similarly to bootstrap).
  settraceprobability [value] - Sets the probability for tracing any given request
                                 to value. 0 disables, 1 enables for all requests,
                                 0 is the default.
```

```
  snapshot [keyspaces...]      - Take a snapshot of the optionally specified column
-cf [columnfamilyName]           family of the specified keyspaces using optional
-t [snapshotName]                name snapshotName.
  clearsnapshot [keyspaces...] - Remove snapshots for the specified keyspaces.
-t [snapshotName]                Either remove all snapshots or remove the
                                 snapshots with the given name.
  flush [keyspace] [cfnames]   - Flush one or more column families.
  repair [keyspace] [cfnames]  - Repair one or more column families (use -pr to
                                 repair only the first range returned by the
                                 partitioner).
  cleanup [keyspace] [cfnames]- Run cleanup on one or more column families.
  compact [keyspace] [cfnames]- Force a (major) compaction on one or more column
                                 families.
  scrub [keyspace] [cfnames]   - Scrub (rebuild sstables for) one or more column
                                 families.
  upgradesstables              - Rewrite sstables (for the requested column families)
[-a|--include-all-sstables]      that are not on the current version (thus upgrading
[keyspace] [cfnames]             them to said current version).
Use                            - a to include all sstables, even those already on
                                 the current version.
  setcompactionthreshold       - Set min and max compaction thresholds for a given
<keyspace> <cfname>              column family.
  getcompactionthreshold       - Print min and max compaction thresholds for a
<keyspace> <cfname>              given column family.
  stop <compaction_type>       - Supported types are COMPACTION, VALIDATION,
                                 CLEANUP, SCRUB, INDEX_BUILD.
  cfhistograms <keyspace>      - Print statistic histograms for a given column
<cfname>                         family.
  refresh <keyspace>           - Load newly placed SSTables to the system without
<cf-name>                        restart.
  rebuild_index <keyspace>     - a full rebuilds of native secondary index for a
<cf-name> <idx1,idx1>            given column family. IndexNameExample: Standard3.
                                 IdxName,Standard3.IdxName1.
  setcachecapacity             - Set global key and row cache capacities (in MB
<key-cache-capacity>             units).
<row-cache-capacity>
  getendpoints <keyspace>      - Print the end points that own the key.
<cf> <key>
  getsstables <keyspace>       - Print the sstable filenames that own the key.
<cf> <key>
  predictconsistency           - Predict latency and consistency "t" ms after
<replication_factor> <time>      writes.
[versions][latency_percentile]
```

We will cover what many of these options do and how to make proper use of them throughout this chapter.

General Usage

While it is common to pass a host to nodetool using the -h or -host switch, if one is not passed, nodetool will assume localhost and run all commands against localhost. All query responses will be from the perspective of the node being queried. So if you want to find out what version of Cassandra the node you are on is running, you can just run `nodetool version` (see Listing 7.2).

Listing 7.2 `nodetool version` **Output**

```
$ nodetool version
ReleaseVersion: 1.2.5
```

Node Information

The first thing you'll want to do when looking into a Cassandra cluster is find out about the individual nodes. To do that, you can run `nodetool info` (see Listing 7.3).

> **Note**
>
> The lack of a `-h` option here implies running it against localhost.

Listing 7.3 `nodetool info` **Output**

```
$ nodetool info
Token            : 113427455640312821154458202477256070484
Gossip active    : true
Thrift active    : true
Load             : 501.29 GB
Generation No    : 1353710956
Uptime (seconds) : 944395
Heap Memory (MB) : 4362.68 / 7088.00
Data Center      : Cassandra
Rack             : rack1
Exceptions       : 0
Key Cache        : size 104857584 (bytes), capacity 104857584 (bytes), 4409164842
                   hits, 4634875698 requests, 0.951 recent hit rate, 14400 save
                   period in seconds
Row Cache        : size 0 (bytes), capacity 0 (bytes), 0 hits, 0 requests, NaN
                   recent hit rate, 0 save period in seconds
```

Most of the items in this output are fairly straightforward. There are a few nuances that should be covered. `Load` references the size of the data on disk. The `Generation No` field is a status report from the Gossip protocol. The number is the time that the most recent heartbeat was received by this node. The `Rack` field is important only if you are using a snitch that makes use of multiple data centers and racks.

Ring Information

The most common command you will probably find yourself running is `nodetool ring`. This command presents all the nodes in the cluster and their status from the perspective of the node being queried. Let's take a look at a healthy and well-balanced three-node cluster (see Listing 7.4).

Listing 7.4 **Healthy Three-Node Ring**

```
$ nodetool ring
  Address        DC        Rack  Status  State            Load     Effective-
                                                                   Ownership Token
                                                                   1134274556403128
                                                                   2115445820247725
                                                                   6070484
  10.100.0.100  us-east  1a    Up      Normal 501.29 MB  33.33%  0
  10.100.1.110  us-east  1a    Up      Normal 441.13 MB  33.33%  5671372782015641
                                                                   0577229101238628
                                                                   035242
  10.100.2.120  us-east  1a    Up      Normal 499.29 MB  33.33%  1134274556403128
                                                                   2115445820247725
                                                                   6070484
```

The columns shown are address, status, state, load, ownership percentage, and tokens. These are all self-explanatory. What you are looking at is the current state of the ring as seen by the querying node.

A few things are worth noting as you look at the output. Notice that the load on each machine is roughly the same, as each owns 33.33% of the data in the ring. The size on disk is different because different data is stored on each node. Additionally, every row must fully fit on one node. If you have wide rows, the more data you get, the more you will see the size in the load section vary from node to node. Last, notice that the last token on the bottom is also the same token listed above the first node. This is the way the wrapping range is displayed.

Since the status on all three nodes is up and the state on all three nodes is normal, we can consider this a healthy ring with some healthy nodes and move on.

ColumnFamily Statistics

In addition to monitoring the health of a node or your cluster, you can also gather some pretty granular statistics using `nodetool`. On the ColumnFamily level, you can run `nodetool cfstats` and see statistics for your cluster at the keyspace and ColumnFamily levels.

Note that you may want to pipe the output through `less` or send the output to a file. Only the keyspace statistics and ColumnFamily statistics are included in Listing 7.5 for a single ColumnFamily in a single keyspace. Each keyspace (including the System Keyspace) and every ColumnFamily within each keyspace will normally be output when this command is run.

Listing 7.5 **Example ColumnFamily Stats Output**

```
$ nodetool cfstats
Keyspace: MainKeyspace
        Read Count: 2032889905
        Read Latency: 2.2192086369876485 ms.
```

(Continues)

Listing 7.5 **Example ColumnFamily Stats Output *(Continued)***

```
        Write Count: 6288511536
        Write Latency: 0.03336843706761708 ms.
        Pending Tasks: 0
                Column Family: events_2013_01
                SSTable count: 12
                Space used (live): 29084623734
                Space used (total): 29084623734
                Number of Keys (estimate): 2513280
                Memtable Columns Count: 345439
                Memtable Data Size: 106877833
                Memtable Switch Count: 1930
                Read Count: 273371162
                Read Latency: 5.695 ms.
                Write Count: 246179400
                Write Latency: 0.070 ms.
                Pending Tasks: 0
                Bloom Filter False Positives: 411
                Bloom Filter False Ratio: 0.00000
                Bloom Filter Space Used: 11691384
                Compacted row minimum size: 61
                Compacted row maximum size: 62479625
                Compacted row mean size: 35204
```

The first thing you'll probably notice is that you get a total read and write count including latencies at the keyspace level. Both of the latency values should be very small numbers in milliseconds, typically less than 1ms. Depending on the current state of the cluster, going up to 4ms or 5ms for read or write latency keyspace-wide may be acceptable. Be sure to keep an eye on the number of pending tasks listed as well. A large number here could be indicative of a larger problem such as resource starvation or hardware issues.

On the ColumnFamily level, read and write latency should also be fairly low values. How low the values are depends on the ColumnFamily and the use case for that ColumnFamily. While it is definitely worth noting what the latencies are, ultimately your query and data storage patterns will dictate what is an acceptable range of values for those latencies.

Thread Pool Statistics

To get access to the statistics on Cassandra thread pools, you can just run `nodetool tpstats` (see Listing 7.6). The overall goal of looking at the thread pool statistics is to see where Cassandra is spending the majority of its time.

Listing 7.6 **Example** `nodetool tpstats` **Output**

```
$ nodetool tpstats
Pool Name                 Active   Pending     Completed   Blocked  All time blocked
ReadStage                      0         0     415352835         0                 0
```

```
RequestResponseStage          0         3  6364673744         0            0
MutationStage                 0         0  6626267281         0            0
ReadRepairStage               0         0    79306899         0            0
ReplicateOnWriteStage         0         0  1358404613         0            0
GossipStage                   0         0    24791245         0            0
AntiEntropyStage              0         0        1648         0            0
MigrationStage                0         0        2370         0            0
MemtablePostFlusher           0         0       32951         0            0
StreamStage                   0         0         141         0            0
FlushWriter                   0         0       34825         0          742
MiscStage                     0         0           0         0            0
commitlog_archiver            0         0           0         0            0
AntiEntropySessions           0         0           7         0            0
InternalResponseStage         0         0        4028         0            0
HintedHandoff                 0         0         129         0            0
Message type            Dropped
RANGE_SLICE                   0
READ_REPAIR                   2
BINARY                        0
READ                          8
MUTATION                    711
REQUEST_RESPONSE              2
```

If you see a lot of zeros in the `Pending` column, you are in one of two situations: either you have very little cluster activity, or your underlying hardware is sufficient for the current load on the cluster. If you see a lot of nonzero values in the `Pending` column, your cluster may be too active for your hardware.

Flushing and Draining

Data coming into the system is temporarily stored in a MemTable. Running `nodetool flush` purges the data from memory (MemTables) and writes it to the disk (SSTables). This also enables older CommitLog segments to be removed. Unlike running a `nodetool drain`, writes are still allowed to the system.

A `flush` is also the first part of a `nodetool drain`. Draining stops the system from accepting writes after the `flush` is complete. Read requests will still be processed. `nodetool drain` is commonly used when the system needs to start up quickly after an upgrade or a restart.

Cleaning

There are many reasons to run `nodetool cleanup`. The most common of these is a change in replication strategy or replication factor. Although these are not common things to do to the cluster, there are certainly situations that warrant either one. After performing the change operation in the CLI (command-line interface) or in CQL, you will come back to the command line and run the cleanup operation. When you run a cleanup from the command line, it will appear as if the command is doing nothing. There is no output on standard out for the command as it runs.

So let's say that you reduced your replication factor from 3 to 2. Now it's time to run the cleanup. What `nodetool cleanup` does is get rid of all the data from the extra copy of the data, thus freeing up space on disk. This is similar to a `nodetool repair` in that it rewrites SSTables, but the goal is slightly different. The goal of a cleanup is just to remove all keys that no longer belong to this node.

Another situation where a cleanup might be used is when moving tokens around. In Cassandra 1.1 and earlier or when vnodes are not used, this would mean changing what tokens are assigned to a particular node or nodes. In Cassandra 1.2 and later, when vnodes are in use, you will need to run a cleanup if the `num_tokens` setting is modified. The reason the cleanup gets run when tokens are moved is that the keys that no longer belong to the node need to be removed.

`upgradesstables` and `scrub`

The reason `nodetool upgradesstables` and `nodetool scrub` are grouped together is that `upgradesstables` is a subset of `scrub`.

The job of `nodetool upgradesstables` is to rebuild your SSTables. This can be done as a result of a version upgrade of Cassandra or something as simple as changing the compression options of a ColumnFamily. When `upgradesstables` runs, it rebuilds all the SSTables and discards data that it deems to be broken.

The additional job that `scrub` does is snapshot your data before rebuilding the SSTables. Although this is a good first step to take, it also means removing the snapshot by hand. If you just want to upgrade your SSTables, it is not necessary to run a `nodetool scrub`.

In the same family of tools as `upgradesstables` and `scrub`, there is a tool that ships with Cassandra called `sstablescrub`. The job of `sstablescrub` is to fix (throw away) corrupted tables. It was designed to be run while the Cassandra node is stopped. You should attempt to run it around the cluster in a rolling fashion. The use of `sstablescrub` is typically not necessary and shouldn't be part of your routine maintenance. It is usually reserved for cases where a `nodetool scrub` failed.

Compactions

The process of merging more files into fewer files is called compaction. This is done for a variety of reasons, ranging from freeing up space to validating data on disk. Compactions are a regular part of working with Cassandra, and the impact can be minimized if handled properly.

What, Where, Why, and How

Cassandra performs multiple types of compactions. Each has its own frequency and its own purpose. The two that we will address are major compactions and minor compactions.

A minor compaction is an automatically triggered compaction that is fired off whenever a new SSTable is created. It attempts to remove tombstones when necessary.

A major compaction is a manually triggered compaction through `nodetool`. It merges/updates the existing SSTables and removes tombstones when necessary.

Both types of compaction mark unneeded SSTables for deletion if required. Either a `nodetool cleanup` or garbage collection will remove the SSTables that are marked for deletion.

Compaction Strategies

There are two kinds of compaction strategies when it comes to ColumnFamilys. In order to get the best performance out of Cassandra on reads, you need to choose the correct compaction strategy for your access pattern. As of Cassandra 1.1, the two types of compaction strategies are SizeTieredCompactionStrategy and LeveledCompactionStrategy.

SizeTieredCompaction

SizeTieredCompactionStrategy is the default strategy in a Cassandra ColumnFamily. If you don't specify a different strategy when creating your ColumnFamily, SizeTieredCompactionStrategy will be used. It is best to use this strategy when you have insert-heavy, read-light workloads. The one thing that is important to keep in mind when using SizeTieredCompactionStrategy is that you have to monitor disk space closely. In the worst of scenarios (in other words, large ColumnFamilys that put you near half the size of your disk), the ColumnFamily can temporarily double in size while compactions are in progress. More is discussed about this in the section on monitoring.

LeveledCompaction

The LeveledCompactionStrategy is a new compaction strategy introduced into Cassandra in the 1.0 release. It is based on (but not an exact implementation of) Google's LevelDB. It is best suited for ColumnFamilys with read-heavy workloads that have frequent updates to existing rows. The key thing to monitor when using LeveledCompaction is read latency. If a node cannot keep up with the write workload and pending compactions as a result of the write workload, read performance will begin to degrade substantially.

If you decide that you want to change the compaction strategy for a ColumnFamily, you can do so with a schema change using the Cassandra-cli.

Listing 7.7 shows an example of a healthy three-node ring.

Listing 7.7 **Healthy Three-Node Ring**

```
ALTER TABLE users
WITH compaction={'class': 'LeveledCompactionStrategy',
                 'sstable_size_in_mb': 160}
```

Impact

When it comes to running compactions, there are a few things to keep in mind. Since minor compactions run automatically, there is nothing to keep track of or think about. When Cassandra needs to run one, it will. But major compactions (especially those run as a result of a nodetool repair) can add a lot of load to the system. Depending on the size of your data and how out of sync it is between replica sets, the length of the repair can range from hours to days.

It is typically best, if possible, to have repairs running during off-peak hours for the cluster. There are even ways to tune the speed of the repair to further take advantage of the repair window. By setting the compaction and streaming thresholds, you can increase the speed at which nodetool performs its work. The default for streaming and compaction is set to 16MB/s. You can change these settings from the command line. If network throughput and disk I/O aren't a problem, unthrottling the compaction throughput and stream throughput may be a good decision.

To unthrottle compactions, run the nodetool command shown in Listing 7.8.

Listing 7.8 **Unthrottling Compaction Speed Using** `nodetool`

```
$ nodetool setcompactionthroughput 0
```

To unthrottle streaming of data between nodes, run the nodetool command shown in Listing 7.9.

Listing 7.9 **Unthrottling Network Traffic Using** `nodetool`

```
$ nodetool setstreamthroughput 0
```

Note that unthrottling streaming on the current node and not unthrottling streaming on the peers that the current node is trying to stream from and to won't help much. If you want to take full advantage of the unthrottled streaming setup, you'll need to run the same command on the node's peers. The way to see which nodes are part of the stream is to run a nodetool netstats and see which hosts the current node has streaming sessions with. You can then use nodetool to unthrottle the other hosts by passing in the host parameter (see Listing 7.10).

Listing 7.10 **Unthrottling Network Traffic Using** `nodetool` **on Multiple Nodes**

```
$ nodetool -h 10.100.1.110 setstreamthroughput 0 &&
  nodetool -h 10.100.2.120 setstreamthroughput 0
```

Don't forget to set the machines back to the throttled compaction and streaming states after the repairs have completed (or the off-peak window has completed). See Listing 7.11 for an example.

Listing 7.11 **Reset the Streaming Throttling Settings**

```
$ nodetool -h localhost setstreamthroughput 16 &&
  nodetool -h localhost setcompactionthroughput 16 &&
  nodetool -h 10.100.1.110 setstreamthroughput 16 &&
  nodetool -h 10.100.2.120 setstreamthroughput 16
```

Backup and Restore

Making backups in Cassandra is a little tricky. The first thing to keep in mind is that in a distributed system, there is likely more than just a lot of data; there are a lot of machines on which the data resides. So whatever you choose as a storage medium for backups, ensure that there is plenty of space.

Are Backups Necessary?

There is some debate as to whether or not backups in a large enough distributed system are even necessary. While it is good practice to make regular backups, it may not be a requirement for your system. And if backups are not a major requirement, the overall complexity and storage requirements for your architecture can be drastically reduced.

There are certain situations where you can get away with not having a backup. But as with any major decision, there are trade-offs. As a reminder, if you have a replication factor of 3, that means you have a copy of data on a total of three separate nodes. In Amazon Web Services terminology, if two of those nodes are in separate availability zones (us-east-1a and us-east-1b) and the third node is in a different region (us-west-1a), the likelihood of all three nodes in that replica set failing is rather low. But since there is still a chance, it is a decision that you have to make based on the data requirements.

Snapshots

The major risk you take with no backup is data problems. And in systems that are bleeding edge and still in heavy development such as Cassandra, there is always a possibility of problems. So let's assume that with your architecture and data set size (or whatever your reasons are) backups are a requirement. In Cassandra, backups are done using snapshots.

When Cassandra data is stored on disk, there are many SSTables per ColumnFamily and many files per table. And that is just on a single node containing a subset of the data. In order to simplify the backup process, the concept of snapshots was created. The purpose of a snapshot is to make a copy of some or all of the data on a node. After the snapshot is created, it can be easily copied or removed from the node for offline storage or anything else for which you may want to use a backup.

There is one major "gotcha" with snapshots; if there is data in the CommitLog, it will not make it into the snapshot. If you want the current data in the CommitLog to be in the snapshot, make sure you run a `nodetool flush` prior to starting the snapshot. As you recall, this will move all the data from the CommitLog into its proper ColumnFamily directories on disk.

Taking Snapshots

Taking a snapshot in Cassandra is a straightforward process that is easily accomplished with `nodetool`. Let's start by creating an unnamed snapshot of the `events` ColumnFamily in our keyspace `MainKeyspace`. This is achieved by running the command shown in Listing 7.12.

Listing 7.12 **Snapshot of `events` ColumnFamily from `MainKeyspace`**

```
$ nodetool snapshot MainKeyspace -cf events
Requested snapshot for: MainKeyspace and column family: events
Snapshot directory: 1361544837468
```

Running this command will accomplish a few things. First, it will perform what is basically a direct file copy of the `events` ColumnFamily into the snapshots subdirectory of the ColumnFamily. The directory created in the previous example is the timestamp in milliseconds at the time the snapshot was taken. The files in this new directory will exactly match all the files in the ColumnFamily directory at the time the snapshot was executed.

Note that it is also possible (and more common) to use the naming feature of `nodetool snapshot` (`-t`) and have the snapshots use a naming convention. For example, if the snapshot in Listing 7.12 were being scripted into a backup system, it would make sense to include the ColumnFamily name, the date and time of the snapshot, and the machine it came from (see Listing 7.13).

Listing 7.13 **Named Snapshot of `events` ColumnFamily from `MainKeyspace`**

```
$ nodetool snapshot MainKeyspace -cf events -t 2013_01_27_14_00_00-events-cs1
Requested snapshot for: MainKeyspace and column family: events
Snapshot directory: 2013_01_27_14_00_00-events-cs1
```

Naming conventions make the programmatic storage and retrieval of backups much easier as well. Another thing to keep in mind is that if you have the drive space, there is no need to move every backup out of the snapshot directory. It is generally a good idea to keep the latest version of each backup in the snapshot directory to maintain the capability to restore quickly if the need arises.

Removing Snapshots

If you are going to keep only the latest snapshot of a particular backup, it would be handy to know how to delete it. Removing snapshots is particularly easy if they are named and named programmatically. If you know that you've taken a snapshot of a few ColumnFamilys in multiple keyspaces with a timestamp as the snapshot name, you can simply issue the command shown in Listing 7.14, and it will iterate over all the ColumnFamilys in all the keyspaces on the machine and remove any snapshot with that name. This includes snapshots of the System Keyspace.

Listing 7.14 **Clear Any Snapshot with the Name 1361544837468**

```
$ nodetool clearsnapshot -t 1361544837468
Requested snapshot for: all keyspaces
```

You can also remove snapshots at a more granular level by keyspace or even by ColumnFamily. To remove the snapshot that we took earlier of the `events` ColumnFamily in the `MainKeyspace`, run the command shown in Listing 7.15.

Listing 7.15 **Removing a Named Snapshot of `events` ColumnFamily from `MainKeyspace`**

```
$ nodetool clearsnapshot MainKeyspace -t 2013_01_27_14_00_00-events-cs1
Requested snapshot for: MainKeyspace
```

CommitLog Archiving

While backups and snapshots are important, there is one fundamental problem with Cassandra snapshots: they are able to back up only the data that has already been flushed from the CommitLogs. With CommitLog archiving, Cassandra now supports point-in-time recovery (available since Cassandra 1.1.1).

To set up a CommitLog segment archive, you first need to find the commitlog_archiving.properties file. It is located in the Cassandra configuration directory; this is usually at /etc/cassandra/conf. Setting up the commitlog_archiving.properties file once you have located it is easy as it requires only four lines. For the `archive_command` and the `restore_command` only one command with arguments is expected or allowed. If you don't want to enable CommitLog archiving, ensure that all the fields in this are left blank or commented out.

`archive_command`

The easiest way to archive a CommitLog segment is with a *nix hard link (see Listing 7.16). Therefore, the `archive_command` parameter should include the fully qualified path name of the segment to archive. The second part of the hard link command is what you want to name the CommitLog archive.

Listing 7.16 **Create a *nix Hard Link to Archive a CommitLog Segment**

```
# ln /raid0/cassandra/commitlogs/ /var/backup/cassandra/commitlogs/1361544837468
```

`restore_command`

After the CommitLog has been archived, it's time to restore it. The `restore_command` parameter is typically something as simple as a *nix copy command (see Listing 7.17).

Listing 7.17 **Copy the Archived CommitLog Segments to the CommitLog Directory**

```
# cp -f /var/backup/cassandra/commitlogs/1361544837468 /raid0/cassandra/commitlogs
```

`restore_directories`

The `restore_directories` parameter is the path to the directory in which the archived CommitLogs are stored (see Listing 7.18).

Listing 7.18 **Example `restore_directories` Path**

```
/var/backup/cassandra/commitlogs/1361544837468
```

`restore_point_in_time`

The format of this parameter is a date and time grouping in the following format: YYYY-MM-DD HH:mm:SS. Note that the hour part of the timestamp should be in 24-hour format (see Listing 7.19).

Listing 7.19 **24-Hour Time Format Example**

```
2013-01-27 13:45:00
```

CommitLog Archiving Notes

There is one "gotcha" with CommitLog archiving. When restoring a CommitLog, the restore stops as soon as the client-supplied timestamp is reached. Since the order in which Cassandra receives mutations and appends them to the CommitLog is not strictly by timestamp, that means that it is possible for some mutations to remain unrecovered.

Since only one command is allowed under the CommitLog archive and restore command sections, the easiest way to get around this is to have the setting point to a script and take parameters. In other words, using a Bash script as the archive command and another Bash script as the restore command, you can programmatically script point-in-time archives and restores of CommitLogs.

Summary

Although Cassandra has the capability to be a set-it-and-forget-it system, it runs most efficiently with a bit of regular care. Depending on some of the design decisions made for your implementation, the amount of maintenance for your cluster may be a lot of work or a little. But figuring out what needs to be done and determining the current state of your system should be done regularly whether you decide to run regular compactions or not. Since most of that can be done with `nodetool`, it is important to have a good understanding of what it can do and what information it can provide.

8

Monitoring

As the old systems adage goes, a service doesn't exist unless it's monitored. In this chapter, we will cover the basics of monitoring Cassandra. These include file-based logging, inspection of the JVM, and monitoring of Cassandra itself.

Logging

Under the covers, Cassandra uses the standard Java log library Log4j. Log4j is another Apache project that enables the capability to control the granularity of log statements using a configuration file. If you want to find out more about what is happening on a particular node than what `nodetool` and JMX MBeans (which we will cover in more detail later in the chapter) are telling you, you can change the logging levels.

As a front end to the Log4j back end, Cassandra uses Simple Logging Façade for Java (SLF4J). The logging levels from least verbose to most verbose are

- `TRACE`
- `DEBUG`
- `INFO`
- `WARN`
- `ERROR`
- `FATAL`

Understanding these logging levels is important not only to help monitor what is going on in the system or on a particular node but also to help troubleshoot problems. In troubleshooting complex systems such as Cassandra, Cassandra's `nodetool`, logging, and even the JMX MBeans can lead to red herrings. So it is necessary to compile as much information pertinent to the problem as possible to help diagnose what might be going on.

Taking a look at a normal healthy Cassandra node's system.log, you will see `INFO` lines that refer to various stages of the system executing their tasks. These include MemTable flushes, HintedHandoffs, and compactions, just to name a few.

Changing Log Levels

If you want to make any changes to the logging schema, you will need to find the log4j-server.properties file. The default logging level for Cassandra and the rootLogger is `INFO`. This level provides a standard amount of information that is sufficient for understanding the general health of your system. It is definitely helpful to see what your system looks like, so you should do so while logging at the `DEBUG` level. Be sure not to leave Cassandra in `DEBUG` mode for production as the entire system will act noticeably slower. To change the standard logging level in Cassandra from `INFO` to `DEBUG`, change the line that looks like this:

```
log4j.rootLogger=INFO,stdout,R
```

to this:

```
log4j.rootLogger=DEBUG,stdout,R
```

Now your Cassandra node will be running in `DEBUG` mode. To change it back, just swap the `INFO` and `DEBUG` again. To show less logging, you can change the logging level to `WARN`, `ERROR`, or `FATAL`.

Example Error

It is worth noting that not all problem messages enter the logs as `WARNING` or higher (higher meaning toward `FATAL`). Listing 8.1 presents an example of when things start to go south. This is a common set of log messages that you may see with your system set at `INFO` level. Even with the logging level set to `INFO`, there is a lot of useful information in the logs. Don't be afraid to keep a regular eye on the logs so you know what patterns of log messages are normal for your system. For example, if things are starting to slow down, you may see something like Listing 8.1.

Listing 8.1 `INFO` Messages That Show Mutation and `READ` Messages Dropped

```
INFO [ScheduledTasks:1]  2012-07-09 20:48:57,290  MessagingService.java (line 607)
3476 MUTATION messages dropped in last5000ms
 INFO [ScheduledTasks:1] 2012-07-09 20:48:57,290 MessagingService.java (line 607)
677 READ messages dropped in last 5000ms
 INFO [ScheduledTasks:1] 2012-07-09 20:48:57,291 StatusLogger.java (line 50)
Pool Name                    Active                    Pending          Blocked
 INFO [ScheduledTasks:1] 2012-07-09 20:48:57,291 StatusLogger.java (line 65)
ReadStage                         32                       621                0
 INFO [ScheduledTasks:1] 2012-07-09 20:48:57,291 StatusLogger.java (line 65)
RequestResponseStage               0                         0                0
 INFO [ScheduledTasks:1] 2012-07-09 20:48:57,291 StatusLogger.java (line 65)
ReadRepairStage                    0                         0                0
 INFO [ScheduledTasks:1] 2012-07-09 20:48:57,291 StatusLogger.java (line 65)
MutationStage                     32                      4105                0
 INFO [ScheduledTasks:1] 2012-07-09 20:48:57,291 StatusLogger.java (line 65)
ReplicateOnWriteStage              0                         0                0
 INFO [ScheduledTasks:1] 2012-07-09 20:48:57,292 StatusLogger.java (line 65)
GossipStage                        0                         0                0
```

```
 INFO [ScheduledTasks:1] 2012-07-09 20:48:57,292 StatusLogger.java (line 65)
AntiEntropyStage                  0                     0            0
 INFO [ScheduledTasks:1] 2012-07-09 20:48:57,292 StatusLogger.java (line 65)
MigrationStage                    0                     0            0
 INFO [ScheduledTasks:1] 2012-07-09 20:48:57,292 StatusLogger.java (line 65)
StreamStage                       0                     0            0
 INFO [ScheduledTasks:1] 2012-07-09 20:48:57,292 StatusLogger.java (line 65)
MemtablePostFlusher               0                     0            0
 INFO [ScheduledTasks:1] 2012-07-09 20:48:57,292 StatusLogger.java (line 65)
FlushWriter                       0                     0            0
 INFO [ScheduledTasks:1] 2012-07-09 20:48:57,292 StatusLogger.java (line 65)
MiscStage                         0                     0            0
 INFO [ScheduledTasks:1] 2012-07-09 20:48:57,292 StatusLogger.java (line 65)
InternalResponseStage             0                     0            0
 INFO [ScheduledTasks:1] 2012-07-09 20:48:57,293 StatusLogger.java (line 65)
HintedHandoff                     1                     8            0
 INFO [ScheduledTasks:1] 2012-07-09 20:48:57,293 StatusLogger.java (line 70)
CompactionManager                 0                     0
 INFO [ScheduledTasks:1] 2012-07-09 20:48:57,293 StatusLogger.java (line 82)
MessagingService                n/a                   0,0
```

When you see messages being dropped, as in the first two lines of the listing, that's a sign that your system is under stress. Depending on your application requirements, some level of dropped messages may be acceptable. But regardless of whether or not your application can tolerate running in a degraded state, the overall health of your cluster (or at the very least this node) is in question. Most applications are capable of handling dropped `READ` requests, but dropped `MUTATION` messages mean that data that should have been written isn't getting written. Depending on the consistency level of the write in question, this could mean the write didn't happen at all, or it could mean the write didn't happen on this node. Also notice that the `ReadStage` and `MutationStage` lines have multiple `Active` and `Pending` messages left to work on. The reason these messages are dropped is that Cassandra wants to do its best to keep up with the volume of work that it is being given.

There are other such common log lines to watch for, which can be done via a log monitor. One method for monitoring the logs programmatically using Nagios will be discussed later in this chapter.

JMX and MBeans

Built into Cassandra and the JVM is the capability to use the JMX, or Java Management Extensions. In other words, using JMX gives you the capability to manage your servers remotely or check into settings programmatically, including the memory, CPU, threads, Gossip, or any other part of the system that has been instrumented in JMX. Instrumentation is what enables the application to provide application-specific information to be collected by external tools. JMX also gives you the ability to control certain aspects of this information.

JConsole

MBeans, or Managed Beans, are a special type of JavaBean that makes a resource inside the application or the JVM available externally. The standard tool that ships with Java for managing the MBeans is JConsole.

The most common use case for accessing a Cassandra server is that the server will be remote and you probably won't have console access to it. It is also highly recommended that you run JConsole remotely as it is a heavy user of resources on a machine and can steal those resources away from the Cassandra node. If this is the case, you can use SSH tunneling to bring up JConsole. When you SSH, be sure to use the `-X` switch to ensure that X11 forwarding is on. This is what enables you to use JConsole over the network. After SSHing into the machine running Cassandra and finding the JConsole binary, just execute it as you would any normal binary. Assuming everything is configured correctly, you will get a JConsole login window as shown in Figure 8.1.

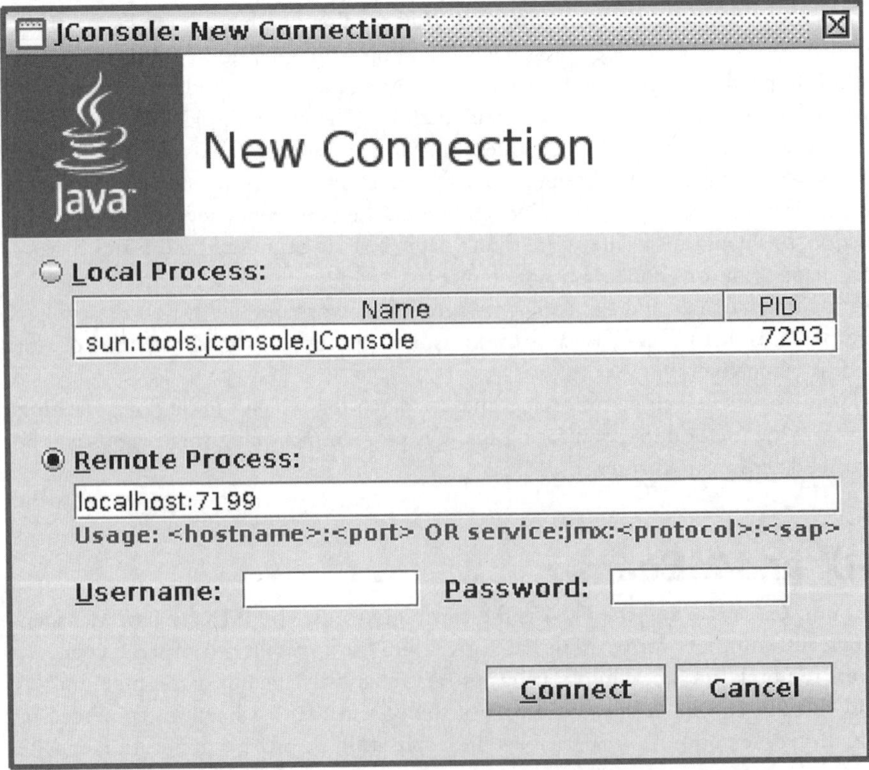

Figure 8.1 JConsole login window when logging in via localhost

Click on the radio button labeled Remote Process and type `localhost:7199`. If you have Cassandra set up with authentication, you will need to put in the username and password as well. Port 7199 is the default JMX port for Cassandra. The first thing you will notice once a connection has been established is that there are multiple tabs that contain information for you to look through. These tabs are Overview, Memory, Threads, Classes, VM Summary, and MBeans.

The Overview, Memory, and Threads tabs are sets of graphs that provide insight into the current state of the system. The Classes graph is simply a graph of how many classes are loaded into the JVM at the current time (or a different time range that you choose). The VM Summary is an overview of what the current view of the Java Virtual Machine is.

Memory

The Memory tab consists of graphs about the current state of the memory (see Figure 8.2). One of the most important memory stats that you want to be aware of is your current heap usage. It is also the default graph that comes up on the Memory tab. As with everything else in your system, it is helpful to know what a good baseline is for heap usage during normal system operations. If you have a 10GB heap set and you find during most of your operations that you are using only 3GB, you can likely reduce your JVM maximum heap size. This will enable you to reduce your memory footprint on the system and possibly even speed up your GCs.

Cassandra also does a lot of work off-heap. Things like bloom filters in version 1.2 and forward are off-heap now. Keeping tabs on what the off-heap memory usage looks like is also very important.

Garbage collection is also one of the metrics that can be viewed from the Memory tab. If needed (though typically not recommended unless you know what you are doing), you can even force a GC from the Memory tab in JConsole. In Cassandra 1.1 and later, there are even helpful bars that display the total memory used versus memory available both on-heap and off-heap.

Threads

The Threads tab in JConsole is dedicated to showing the current and peak usage patterns of various thread stages in Cassandra (see Figure 8.3). These include everything that you would normally see in the logs from things like the CommitLog handler and compaction scheduler all the way to garbage collection, Gossip, and streaming. It is also helpful here to see how many threads your system uses normally as well as under load.

MBeans

The final tab in JConsole is the tab for MBeans (see Figure 8.4). There are a lot of MBeans that are useful for assessing the state of your Cassandra node and your Cassandra cluster. You will notice that there are a few groupings here that can be expanded. Other than the standard Java MBeans that are available to every agent, there are several groupings specific to Cassandra. All of their class paths start with org.apache.cassandra.

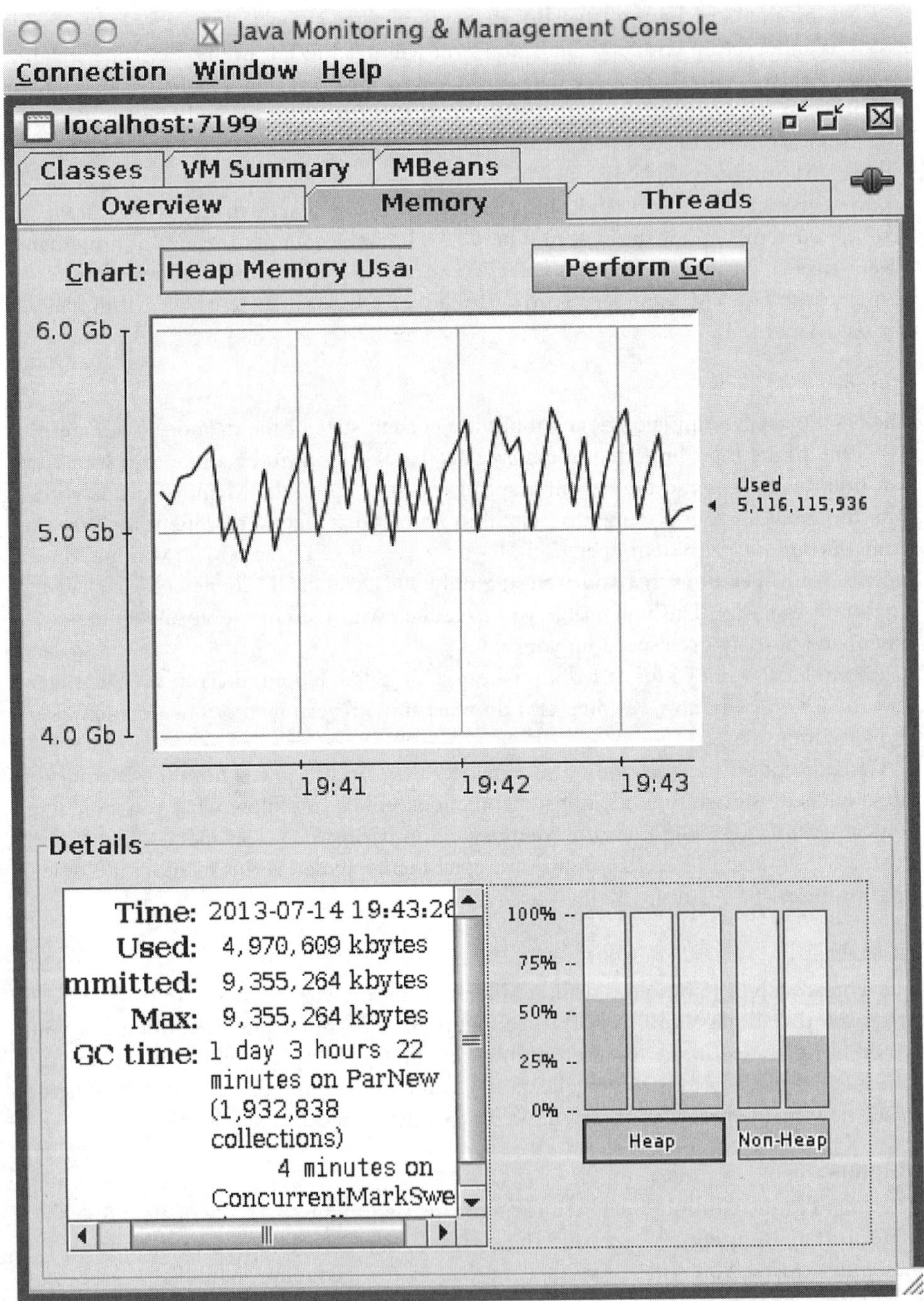

Figure 8.2 JConsole Memory tab displaying heap usage graphs

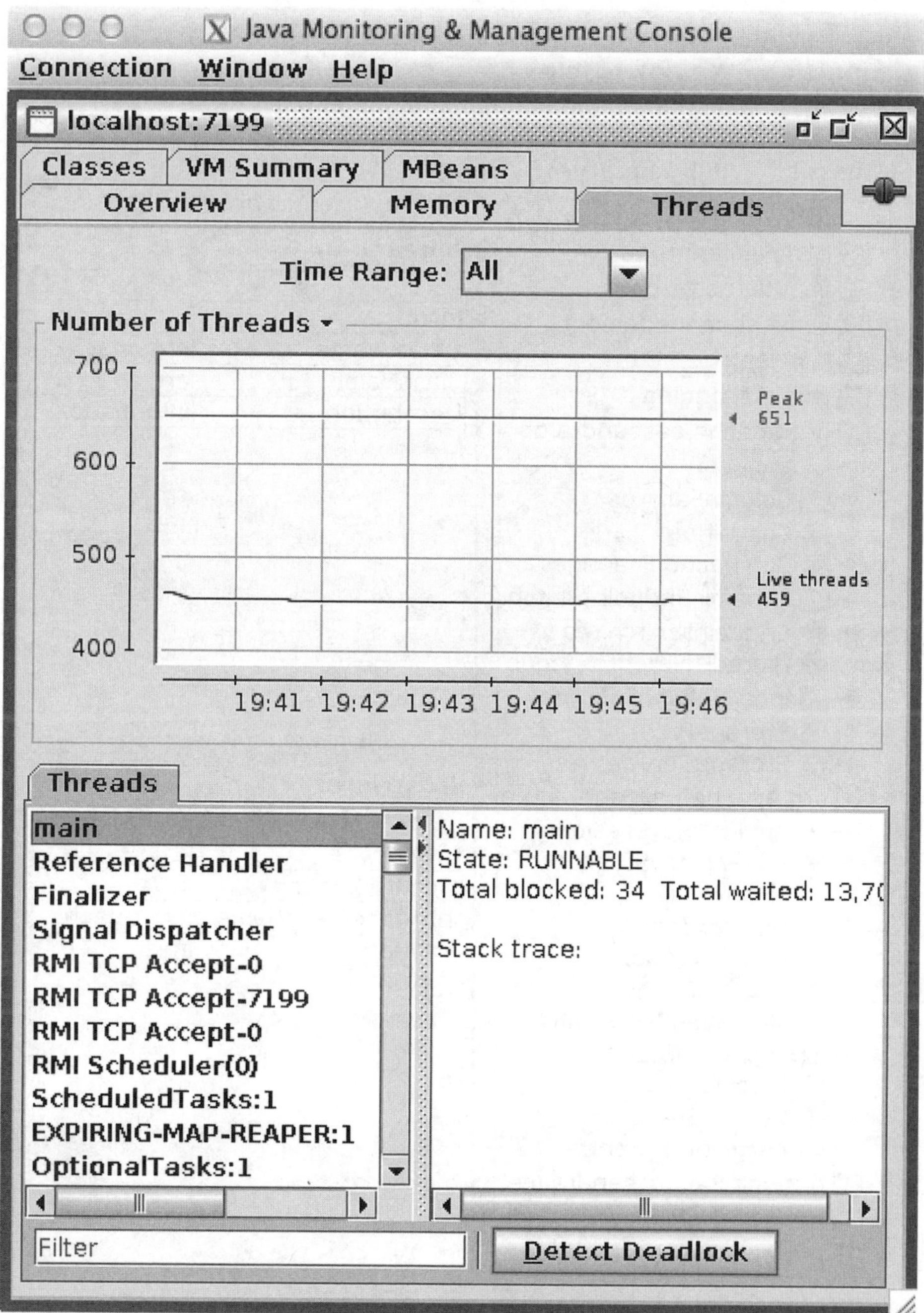

Figure 8.3 JConsole Threads tab displaying the number of threads Cassandra is currently using and general information on the main Cassandra thread

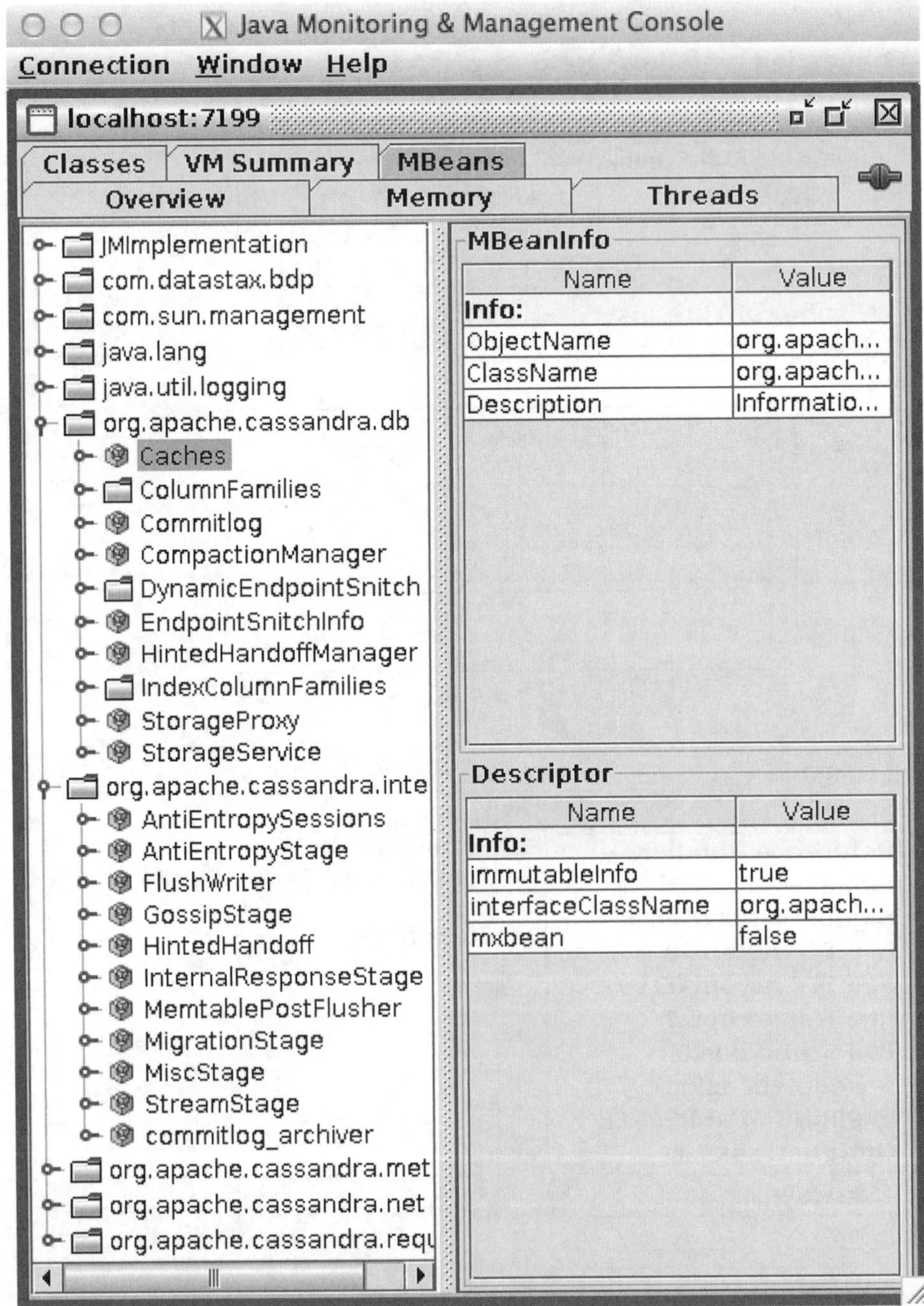

Figure 8.4 JConsole MBeans tab view with the Cassandra DB and Internal trees opened

There are a lot of MBeans provided by an application as complex as Cassandra. There is no need to cover all of them as you can easily explore them on your own using the JConsole interface.

As a high-level overview, they are broken down into the following categories:

- **DB.** The MBeans stored in the DB section cover everything about the actual data storage part of Cassandra. You can view information about the cache and CommitLogs, or even information about the individual ColumnFamilys that you have created in each of the keyspaces. HintedHandoffManager, EndPointSnitchInfo, and CompactionManager information can also be found here.
- **Internal.** In the Internal section, there are MBeans that cover the state and statistics around the staged architecture. More specifically, you can find information about the state of Gossip and HintedHandoff as opposed to just finding information about the managers as in the DB section.
- **Metrics.** The metrics available in this section are ClientRequestMetrics. These are things like read and write timeouts and `Unavailable` errors.
- **Net.** The network section houses information about internode communication. This includes information about the FailureDetector, Gossiper, MessagingService, and StreamingService.
- **Request.** The MBeans in the Request section are about tasks related to read, write, and replication.

When you select any MBean in the tree, its MBeanInfo and MBean descriptor are displayed on the right-hand side of the window. If any additional attributes, operations, or notifications are available, they will appear in the tree as well, below the selected MBean.

Each one of these sections of MBeans provides access to a large amount of information, giving you insight into both the system as a whole and the individual nodes. Familiarizing yourself with what is available to you as an admin will help you when it comes time to instrument JMX-level checks from within your monitoring system.

Health Checks

Using JConsole to monitor your system is tedious and good as a monitoring system only if you are actively staring at the graphs and information all the time. Since that is unrealistic and time-consuming, we recommend that you use other systems for monitoring the general health of your system such as Nagios.

Nagios

Nagios is open-source software dedicated to monitoring computers, networks, hosts, and services and can alert you when things are going wrong or have been resolved. It is extremely versatile and has the capability to monitor many types of services, applications, or parts of an application. Let's start at the bottom of the monitoring chain and work our way up. In order to avoid a complete lesson on monitoring, we will only cover the basics along with what the most common checks should be as they relate to Cassandra and its operation.

There are three primary alerts in Nagios: `WARNING`, `CRITICAL`, and `OK`. They mean exactly what they sound like. A `WARNING` alert is sent if the service in question is starting to show signs of a problem, such as a hard drive nearing capacity. A `CRITICAL` alert is sent if the service in question is down or in a catastrophic state, such as a hard drive that is completely out of space and preventing the applications using that drive from running. An `OK` alert is sent when the service has recovered or become available again, such as when the total space used on the hard drive has dropped below the threshold set to alert for `CRITICAL` or `WARNING`.

OS and Hardware Checks

When monitoring any machine, it's best to start out with the checks at the OS and hardware layer. Even if you are running Cassandra in a virtualized environment such as Amazon or Rackspace, there are still hardware(ish) checks that should be instituted.

Disks and Partitions

The first thing you are going to want to check is the amount of free disk space on data partitions and the CommitLog partitions (assuming they are on separate partitions). Remember that if you are using SizeTieredCompaction, you shouldn't have the alert set for `WARNING` at 80% disk utilization and `CRITICAL` set at 90% disk utilization. The safer approach is to set the `WARNING` threshold to be roughly 35% disk utilization and the `CRITICAL` threshold at 45% disk utilization. SizeTieredCompaction is capable of taking up two times the size of the largest SSTable on disk. And while it is unlikely that a single SSTable would be 50% of the data on disk, it is better to be safe than sorry. Recovering from having too much data on disk is extremely difficult.

This concept of monitoring partitions and drives is also important because of JBoD support in Cassandra 1.2 and later. This means that Cassandra can have a single data directory on multiple disks. You will need to know if one or more of those disks are having an issue or require replacement. By monitoring the utilization and health of all the disks in your system, you will know their state and whether they need replacing or maintenance.

Last, you want to ensure that the drive that contains the log files doesn't fill up. Depending on your log settings, Cassandra has the potential to be very verbose in the log files. If the log files become too large, they can prevent the rest of your system from working if the drive(s) runs out of space.

Swap

Linux divides its physical memory into smaller chunks called pages. Swapping is the process whereby a page of memory is copied from memory to a dedicated space on the hard disk called swap space to free up that page of memory. Although there are cases where it is OK, it is normally not recommended for systems to be in a state where they are swapping memory. Typically, anything more than 5% to 10% of your swap space being used is cause for investigation.

On a Cassandra node, swapping is usually a bad sign, so you will want to monitor the swap partition for usage of nearly any kind. Since you should be able to hold the entire JVM's heap space in memory with at least a little room to spare for the operating system, getting to the point of swapping out pages of memory means it might be a little too late to recover. One of the reasons Cassandra is able to function so well with regard to writes is the fact that many of the writes occur to the memory-mapped MemTables. Having these MemTables swap to disk would drastically impair the performance of Cassandra and should therefore be avoided when possible.

Clock Drift

Clock drift refers to the phenomenon where one clock does not run at the exact same speed as another clock. It is especially important to be aware of this if you are running in a virtualized environment as drift from the hypervisor can be much more prevalent than on regular iron. The system clock is incredibly important to Cassandra's write and reconciliation architecture. Most writes are serialized by timestamp. In other words, if two writes come in for the same column at almost the same time, the determining factor for which value wins is which timestamp is higher. If the system clocks in the ring are not all in sync, you are probably going to see some really strange behavior.

One of the ways to deal with that is to monitor the clock drift using NTP. NTP, or Network Time Protocol, is the most commonly used time synchronization system on the Internet. It also comes with a binary for telling you the offset (drift) from its synchronizing time server. You obviously want to minimize the amount of drift your system experiences. But there will invariably be some that you have to deal with. Monitoring is the way you know if the NTP daemon isn't doing the job it is supposed to be doing and keeping your clocks in sync. Being alerted to a problem with the clocks in a distributed environment that relies heavily on time for decision making could save a lot of time tracking down weird problems later on.

Ping Times

It is also a good idea to check the ping time responses from each of the Cassandra nodes being monitored. There are any number of reasons that these responses can begin to come back slowly. A few examples include the following:

- A machine that is doing too much work and running short of CPU cycles to respond quickly
- I/O saturation, too high an await (average wait) time, and the machine cannot respond quickly to the request
- Network saturation due to unthrottled streaming on a high-speed network link

Whatever the reason is, it is good to know if there is network congestion of which you should be aware. When a node is slow to receive packets (which is the case with nodes with high ping times), writes can be slow to come in and register, reads and writes will be dropped to keep up with the demand being put on the system, or any number of other weird behaviors may appear. What constitutes a high ping time from your monitoring server depends to a great extent on your network paths. Run a few ping tests from your monitoring server to your Cassandra nodes during regular usage periods to get a feel for what a normal threshold is.

CPU Usage

Cassandra is usually an I/O-bound system. You usually run into problems with disk writes or reads slowing down long before you run into CPU-related slowdown. But just to be safe, as different workloads call for different tools to be used at different times, you should monitor CPU usage. While there are many things you could look for when monitoring CPU usage, such as context switches or interrupt requests, a good place to start is usually watching the system load average. The system load average is an average of the number of processes waiting to get into the system's run queue over a period of time. In the case of the `uptime` command, it's over one, five, and 15 minutes. Keep in mind that in the case of multiprocessor systems, the load is relative to the number of processors and cores on the system.

The common rule for utilization is that you want to have a machine working hard but not overworking. This means that you typically want to have the machine running at about 70% utilization. That leaves you headroom for spikes in work and doesn't leave the machine underutilized during slower periods. So if you have four cores, having the load sit at around 3.00 is usually a safe bet. If you have four cores and the load is 3.5 or higher, you should try to find out what's wrong and fix it before things go from bad to worse.

Cassandra-Specific Health Checks

Once you have the basic system checks in place, it's time to add monitoring that is specific to Cassandra. There are various checks that interact with Cassandra at different levels of the system. Some are superficial such as checking to see if ports are alive and being listened on. Some checks require using a slightly more in-depth toolset to programmatically check the MBeans described earlier.

Ports

There are three primary ports of interest to Cassandra: 7000 (or 7001 if SSL/TLS is enabled), 7199, and 9160. Port 7000/7001 is used by Cassandra for cluster communication. This includes things such as the Gossip protocol and failure detection. Port 7199 is used by JMX. Port 9160 is the Thrift port and is used for client communication. In order for your cluster to function properly, all of these ports should be accessible.

While it is not necessary to specifically monitor these ports, it is a good idea to test them out one way or another. Testing the Thrift port (9160) is just testing whether you can connect to an instance using a Cassandra driver. In terms of monitoring, if you can connect, the check passes. If you can't connect to the server, the check should send off an alert. You can also use a simple TCP check here even though it is less comprehensive.

JMX Checks

Using some of the knowledge we gained from looking at the normal behavior of our system with JConsole, we are going to add some checks using JMX. There are plug-ins for Nagios that enable you to run JMX queries and compare the results against a set of predetermined thresholds. While there are many values that can be monitored through JMX, there are a few that stand out.

The first set of JMX checks to create is for read and write request latency. These values are given in microseconds because they should be that small. These latencies can be measured at the Cassandra application level and/or at the ColumnFamily level. Measuring them at the application level is important as a general health metric. High request latencies can be indicative of a bad disk or that your current read pattern is starting to slow down. If there is a ColumnFamily for which it is particularly important to have extremely low-latency reads and/or writes, it would be a good decision to monitor the performance for that ColumnFamily as well. It is important to note that read latency and write latency are two separate metrics provided by Cassandra, and both are important in their own right depending on your workload.

The next set of JMX metrics to keep tabs on is garbage collection timing. Cassandra will not only tell you how long its last garbage collection took but also how long that last ParNew GC took. A good way to think of ParNew garbage collection is that it is a stop-the-world garbage collection that uses multiple GC threads to complete its job. If you are monitoring the amount of time these take, you can easily set up an alert for when they start to take too long. Cassandra is unavailable during a stop-the-world garbage collection pause. The longer these pauses take, the longer Cassandra will be unavailable.

Another metric that is useful in helping to determine whether or not you need to add capacity to your cluster is PendingTasks under the CompactionManagerMBean. Depending on the speed and volume with which you ingest data, you will need to find a comfortable set of thresholds for your system. Typically, the number of PendingTasks should be relatively low, as in fewer than 50 at any given time. There are certainly acceptable reasons for things to back up, such as forced compactions or cleanup, but it is advisable to watch this metric carefully. If you have an alert set for PendingTasks and find this alert firing regularly, you may need to add more capacity (either more or faster disks or more nodes) to your cluster to keep up with the workload.

The last JMX metrics that should make it onto your first round of monitoring are the amount of on-heap and the amount of off-heap memory used at a time. The amount of on-heap memory used should always be less than the amount of heap that you have allowed the JVM to allocate. Since you know what this value is at start time, you should be able to easily monitor whether or not you are approaching that value. Off-heap memory tracking is a little harder to monitor for sane values. This is a metric where you will once again have to take a look at JConsole and see what regular and peak values are for the system under normal and peak operational loads so you don't send off useless alerts.

Log Monitoring

There is a lot of useful information in the Cassandra logs that can be indicative of a problem. As mentioned earlier in the chapter, you can find `READ` and `WRITE` dropped message counts within the `INFO` log level. There is a Nagios plug-in that can monitor logs and check for specific log messages. Using this plug-in, you can have Nagios alert you not just when there are `READ` and/or `WRITE` messages dropped, but you also can have it alert you when this happens more than *n* times per period. For instance, your application may be tolerant of missing `READ`s and much less tolerant of missing `WRITE`s. So the log monitoring check can alert you with a `CRITICAL` alert if more than 1,000 mutations have been dropped over a five-minute period and with a WARNING alert if more than 1,000 mutations have been dropped over a 15-minute period.

This is just in the case of bad things happening in the INFO level. You can also have the log monitoring system alert you if any FATAL, ERROR, or WARNING log messages are put into the logs. Many of these plug-ins are configurable enough to send the log messages (or at least the one that caused the notification) along with the alert.

Cassandra Interactions

Now that we have the OS and system layer monitored and we know Cassandra is up and at least responding, it's time to check a little deeper. The further into the application you monitor, the better you will be able to sleep at night knowing things are functioning the way you want them to. Although it is useful and necessary to have superficial checks like load average and memory, the real value of monitoring systems is realized as you get deeper into the application.

What this means is that you should be checking things that are specific to your application in addition to the Cassandra server. If your application writes to a new ColumnFamily at the beginning of every month, you should have your monitoring system check before the month turnover that the new ColumnFamily exists (and optionally create it if it doesn't).

Another good use of monitoring resources is to check the response time of certain queries. If you are regularly running queries that roll up all the events for an hour, monitor how long that query takes to run and set up an alert if it's outside the normal threshold. In other words, if the query runs too fast, you want to know because it's possible you aren't collecting all the data you expect to be there. If the query takes too long to run, your system could be under heavy load or you may have just hit a point where you need to rethink your query patterns. Either way, that type of instrumentation is useful to measure how your system actually performs compared to how you expect it to perform.

If you run an application at the top of every hour—an extract, transform, load (ETL) process, for example—it might be a good idea to have the application put a "run complete" column somewhere when it's done. At the beginning of every hour, the monitoring system can run a query to check for the existence of the column for the last hour. If the "run complete" column doesn't exist for the last hour, it would be good to know so you can look into why.

Summary

There are many tools available for building monitoring systems. Nagios is just one of the common general-purpose monitoring tools. As long as some application is checking on the health and availability of your system and letting you know when an issue is present, or about to present itself, you will be in good shape. There are also some good examples of how your main application and other parts of your application interact with Cassandra and can be instrumented to give you a feeling of total information awareness and potentially the ability to get a good night's sleep when it is all in production.

In this example, Nagios can act as an early-warning tool. It can give you a heads-up to look at the machine in question and dig deeper into a potential problem before it turns into something more serious such as a full-fledged outage or a completely downed node. Ensuring an intelligently set-up monitoring infrastructure is essential to having a well-designed and architected system.

9

Drivers and Sample Code

In this chapter, we will present some of the clients for the most popular languages. Using the most recent driver for each of the languages, we will outline how to connect to a Cassandra cluster, initiate a session, execute CQL queries, and close the connection to the cluster.

There are currently quite a few drivers for Cassandra. Table 9.1 shows the most popular currently maintained drivers; their support of CQL, CBP (CQL Binary Protocol), and Thrift; and where to get them.

Table 9.1 **Various Clients**

Driver	CQL	CBP	Thrift	URL
java-driver	Yes	Yes	No	https://github.com/datastax/java-driver
python-driver	Yes	Yes	No	https://github.com/datastax/python-driver
csharp-driver	Yes	Yes	No	https://github.com/datastax/csharp-driver
cql-rb	Yes	Yes	No	https://github.com/iconara/cql-rb
Hector	No	No	Yes	https://github.com/hector-client/hector
Astyanax	Yes	No	Yes	https://github.com/Netflix/astyanax
Pycassa	No	No	Yes	https://github.com/pycassa/pycassa
PHPCassa	No	No	Yes	https://github.com/thobbs/phpcassa
libQtCassandra	No	No	Yes	http://snapwebsites.org/project/libqtcassandra
Helenus	Yes	No	Yes	https://github.com/simplereach/helenus

Clients that currently support the CQL 3 Binary Protocol also support automatic node failure detection, as well as node failover and node load balancing. DataStax-maintained drivers also come with optional smart load balancing for keyspaces that use the Murmur3Partitioner. The smart load balancing will always choose a coordinator node that is part of the replica set for that query; this gives a slight performance improvement.

For more drivers and information on support for various languages and features, planetcassandra.org is constantly maintained and has plenty of Cassandra drivers, resources, and tutorials for getting started.

Java

Though there are several Java drivers out there, the current driver that fully supports the CQL 3 Binary Protocol is the driver distributed by DataStax. Using your preferred IDE, you need to first add `com.datastax.driver` as a dependency to your project.

To start the example, we will first create an empty class with a private cluster variable and import our required packages. Listing 9.1 outlines how to import the required packages and create our sample class.

Listing 9.1 **Creating the Sample Java Class**

```
package com.example.cassandra;

import com.datastax.driver.core.Cluster;
import com.datastax.driver.core.Host;
import com.datastax.driver.core.Metadata;
import com.datastax.driver.core.Session;
import com.datastax.driver.core.ResultSet;
import com.datastax.driver.core.Row;
public class SampleApp {
  private Cluster cluster;
  private Session session;
}
```

Connecting

When connecting to the cluster, we need to specify only a single node. The driver will automatically query for information about the cluster and build a connection to each of the nodes in the cluster. Listing 9.2 shows how to connect to a cluster and print out information about the connections to the cluster.

Listing 9.2 **Using Java to Connect to a Cluster**

```
public void connect(String node) {
  cluster = Cluster.builder().addContactPoint(node).build();
  Metadata metadata = cluster.getMetadata();
  System.out.printf("Cluster: %s\n", metadata.getClusterName());
   for ( Host host : metadata.getAllHosts() ) {
     System.out.printf("Host: %s \n",host.getAddress());
   }
  session = cluster.connect();
}
```

Disconnecting

To disconnect from the cluster, all you need to do is call `shutdown` on the cluster object. Listing 9.3 shows how to do this.

Listing 9.3 **Using Java to Disconnect from a Cluster**

```
public void close(){
  cluster.shutdown();
}
```

Schema Creation

Now that all of the connections have been created, we can create our schema. When creating the schema, we can use the optional `IF NOT EXISTS` conditional, which will allow running the command multiple times without error. When this conditional is not specified, additional executions of the schema creation code will result in a `QueryExecutionException`. This conditional is available only in Cassandra 2.0 and later. Listing 9.4 shows how to create a keyspace and a sample table.

Listing 9.4 **Creating a Schema in Java**

```
public void createSchema(){
  session.execute("CREATE KEYSPACE IF NOT EXISTS portfolio_demo " +
                "WITH REPLICATION = { 'class': 'SimpleStrategy', " +
                "'replication_factor': 1 };");

  session.execute("CREATE TABLE IF NOT EXISTS portfolio (" +
                "portfolio_id UUID, ticker TEXT, " +
                "current_price DECIMAL, current_change DECIMAL, " +
                "current_change_percent FLOAT, " +
                "PRIMARY KEY(portfolio_id, ticker);");
}
```

Writing Data

Once our schema has been created, we can load in some data. In this example, we will add a couple of rows to our table. Listing 9.5 shows example insert statements.

Listing 9.5 **Writing Data in Java**

```
public void loadData(){
  session.execute("INSERT INTO portfolio_demo.portfolio " +
                "(portfolio_id, ticker, current_price, " +
                " current_change, current_change_percent) VALUES " +
                "(756716f7-2e54-4715-9f00-91dcbea6cf50, 'GOOG', " +
                " 889.07, -4.00, -0.45);");
  session.execute("INSERT INTO portfolio_demo.portfolio " +
                "(portfolio_id, ticker, current_price, " +
```

(Continues)

Listing 9.5 **Writing Data in Java *(Continued)***

```
                    " current_change, current_change_percent) VALUES " +
                    "(756716f7-2e54-4715-9f00-91dcbea6cf50, 'AMZN', " +
                    " 297.92, -0.94, -0.31);");
}
```

Reading Data

When reading data, the query execution will return an instance of `ResultSet` that will allow access to the values of the fields requested. Listing 9.6 shows query execution and printing the results to the console.

Listing 9.6 **Reading Data in Java**

```
public void printResults(){
  ResultSet results = session.execute("SELECT * FROM " +
      "portfolio_demo.portfolio WHERE portfolio_id = " +
      "756716f7-2e54-4715-9f00-91dcbea6cf50;");

  for (Row row : results) {
    System.out.println(String.format("%-7s\t%-7s\t%-7s\t%-7s \n%s",
        "Ticker", "Price", "Change", "PCT",
        "........+........+........+........"));

    System.out.println(String.format("%-7s\t%0.2f\t%0.2f\t%0.2f",
        row.getString("ticker"),
        row.getDecimal("current_price"),
        row.getDecimal("current_change"),
        row.getFloat("current_change_percent") ));
  }
}
```

Putting It All Together

Listing 9.7 shows the entire sample class as it would look in an application.

Listing 9.7 **Full Java Sample**

```
package com.example.cassandra;

import com.datastax.driver.core.Cluster;
import com.datastax.driver.core.Host;
import com.datastax.driver.core.Metadata;
import com.datastax.driver.core.Session;
import com.datastax.driver.core.ResultSet;
import com.datastax.driver.core.Row;

public class SampleApp {
  private Cluster cluster;
  private Session session;
```

```
public void connect(String node) {
  cluster = Cluster.builder().addContactPoint(node).build();
  Metadata metadata = cluster.getMetadata();
  System.out.printf("Cluster: %s\n", metadata.getClusterName());
  for ( Host host : metadata.getAllHosts() ) {
    System.out.printf("Host: %s \n",host.getAddress());
  }
  session = cluster.connect();
}

public void close(){
  cluster.shutdown();
}

public void createSchema(){
  session.execute("CREATE KEYSPACE IF NOT EXISTS portfolio_demo " +
      "WITH REPLICATION = { 'class': 'SimpleStrategy', " +
      "'replication_factor': 1 };");

  session.execute("CREATE TABLE IF NOT EXISTS portfolio_demo.portfolio (" +
      "portfolio_id UUID, ticker TEXT, " +
      "current_price DECIMAL, current_change DECIMAL, " +
      "current_change_percent FLOAT, " +
      "PRIMARY KEY(portfolio_id, ticker));");
}

public void loadData(){
  session.execute("INSERT INTO portfolio_demo.portfolio " +
      "(portfolio_id, ticker, current_price, " +
      " current_change, current_change_percent) VALUES " +
      "(756716f7-2e54-4715-9f00-91dcbea6cf50, 'GOOG', " +
      " 889.07, -4.00, -0.45);");
  session.execute("INSERT INTO portfolio_demo.portfolio " +
      "(portfolio_id, ticker, current_price, " +
      " current_change, current_change_percent) VALUES " +
      "(756716f7-2e54-4715-9f00-91dcbea6cf50, 'AMZN', " +
      " 297.92, -0.94, -0.31);");
}

public void printResults(){
  ResultSet results = session.execute("SELECT * FROM " +
      "portfolio_demo.portfolio WHERE portfolio_id = " +
      "756716f7-2e54-4715-9f00-91dcbea6cf50;");

  for (Row row : results) {
    System.out.println(String.format("%-7s\t%-7s\t%-7s\t%-7s \n%s",
        "Ticker", "Price", "Change", "PCT",
        "........+........+........+........"));
```

(Continues)

Listing 9.7 **Full Java Sample *(Continued)***

```
      System.out.println(String.format("%-7s\t%0.2f\t%0.2f\t%0.2f",
          row.getString("ticker"),
          row.getDecimal("current_price"),
          row.getDecimal("current_change"),
          row.getFloat("current_change_percent") ));
    }
  }

  public static void main(String[] args) {
    SampleApp client = new SampleApp();
    client.connect("127.0.0.1");
    client.createSchema();
    client.loadData();
    client.printResults();
    client.close();
  }
}
```

C#

The C# driver uses the CQL 3 Binary Protocol and is currently maintained by DataStax. To get started, first create a new console application in C# using .NET Framework 4.5. In the Package Manager Console window, type `Install-Package CassandraCSharpDriver`.

To start this example, we will first need to include our `using` directives so that we have access to our Cassandra driver. We will then namespace our application and create our class. We will also add a private instance variable for our cluster and our session. Listing 9.8 shows the class creation.

Listing 9.8 **Creating a Sample C# Class**

```
using Cassandra;
using System;
namespace CassandraExample {
  class SampleApp {
    private Cluster cluster;
    private Session session;
  }
}
```

Connecting

When connecting to the cluster, we need to specify only a single node. The driver will automatically query for information about the cluster and build a connection to each of the nodes in the cluster. Listing 9.9 shows how to connect to a cluster and print out information about the connections to the cluster.

Listing 9.9 **Using C# to Connect to a Cluster**

```
public void Connect(String node) {
  cluster = Cluster.Builder().AddContactPoint(node).Build();
  session = cluster.Connect();
  Metadata metadata = cluster.Metadata;
  Console.WriteLine("Cluster: " + metadata.ClusterName.ToString());
  foreach (Host host in metadata.AllHosts()) {
    Console.WriteLine("Host: " + host.Address);
  }
}
```

Disconnecting

To disconnect from the cluster, all you need to do is call `Shutdown` on the cluster object. Listing 9.10 shows how to do this.

Listing 9.10 **Using C# to Disconnect from a Cluster**

```
public void Close() {
  cluster.Shutdown();
}
```

Schema Creation

Now that all of the connections have been created, we can create our schema. When creating the schema, we can use the optional `IF NOT EXISTS` conditional, which will allow running the command multiple times without error. When this conditional is not specified, additional executions of the schema creation code will result in a `QueryExecutionException`. This conditional is available only in Cassandra 2.0 and later. Listing 9.11 shows how to create a keyspace and a sample table.

Listing 9.11 **Creating a Schema in C#**

```
public void CreateSchema() {
  session.Execute("CREATE KEYSPACE IF NOT EXISTS portfolio_demo " +
        "WITH REPLICATION = { 'class': 'SimpleStrategy', " +
        "'replication_factor': 1 };");

  session.Execute("CREATE TABLE IF NOT EXISTS portfolio_demo.portfolio (" +
      "portfolio_id UUID, ticker TEXT, " +
      "current_price DECIMAL, current_change DECIMAL, " +
      "current_change_percent FLOAT, " +
      "PRIMARY KEY(portfolio_id, ticker));");
}
```

Writing Data

Once our schema has been created, we can load in some data. In this example, we will add a couple of rows to our table. Listing 9.12 shows example insert statements.

Listing 9.12 **Writing Data in C#**

```
public void LoadData() {
  session.Execute("INSERT INTO portfolio_demo.portfolio " +
      "(portfolio_id, ticker, current_price, " +
      " current_change, current_change_percent) VALUES " +
      "(756716f7-2e54-4715-9f00-91dcbea6cf50, 'GOOG', " +
      " 889.07, -4.00, -0.45);");
  session.Execute("INSERT INTO portfolio_demo.portfolio " +
      "(portfolio_id, ticker, current_price, " +
      " current_change, current_change_percent) VALUES " +
      "(756716f7-2e54-4715-9f00-91dcbea6cf50, 'AMZN', " +
      " 297.92, -0.94, -0.31);");
}
```

Reading Data

When reading data, the query execution will return an instance of `ResultSet` that will allow access to the values of the fields requested. Listing 9.13 shows query execution and printing the results to the console.

Listing 9.13 **Reading Data in C#**

```
public void PrinResults() {
  RowSet results = session.Execute("SELECT * FROM " +
    "portfolio_demo.portfolio WHERE portfolio_id = " +
    "756716f7-2e54-4715-9f00-91dcbea6cf50;");

  Console.WriteLine(String.Format("{0, -7}\t{1, -7}\t{2, -7}\t{3, -7}\r\n{4}",
    "Ticker", "Price", "Change", "PCT",
    "........+........+........+........"));

  foreach (Row row in results.GetRows()) {
    Console.WriteLine(String.Format("{0, -7}\t{1, -7}\t{2, -7}\t{3, -7}",
      row.GetValue@String:("ticker"),
      row.GetValue@Decimal:("current_price"),
      row.GetValue@Decimal:("current_change"),
      row.GetValue@float:("current_change_percent")));
  }
}
```

Putting It All Together

Listing 9.14 shows the entire sample class as it would look in an application.

Listing 9.14 **Full C# Sample**

```
using Cassandra;
using System;
```

```
namespace CassandraExample {
  class SampleApp {
    private Cluster cluster;
    private Session session;

    public void Connect(String node) {
      cluster = Cluster.Builder().AddContactPoint(node).Build();
      session = cluster.Connect();
      Metadata metadata = cluster.Metadata;
      Console.WriteLine("Cluster: " + metadata.ClusterName.ToString());
      foreach (Host host in metadata.AllHosts()) {
        Console.WriteLine("Host: " + host.Address);
      }
    }

    public void Close() {
      cluster.Shutdown();
    }

    public void CreateSchema() {

      session.Execute("CREATE KEYSPACE IF NOT EXISTS portfolio_demo " +
            "WITH REPLICATION = { 'class': 'SimpleStrategy', " +
            "'replication_factor': 1 };");

      session.Execute("CREATE TABLE IF NOT EXISTS portfolio_demo.portfolio (" +
          "portfolio_id UUID, ticker TEXT, " +
          "current_price DECIMAL, current_change DECIMAL, " +
          "current_change_percent FLOAT, " +
          "PRIMARY KEY(portfolio_id, ticker));");
    }

    public void LoadData() {
      session.Execute("INSERT INTO portfolio_demo.portfolio " +
          "(portfolio_id, ticker, current_price, " +
          " current_change, current_change_percent) VALUES " +
          "(756716f7-2e54-4715-9f00-91dcbea6cf50, 'GOOG', " +
          " 889.07, -4.00, -0.45);");
      session.Execute("INSERT INTO portfolio_demo.portfolio " +
          "(portfolio_id, ticker, current_price, " +
          " current_change, current_change_percent) VALUES " +
          "(756716f7-2e54-4715-9f00-91dcbea6cf50, 'AMZN', " +
          " 297.92, -0.94, -0.31);");
    }
```

(Continues)

Listing 9.14 **Full C# Sample *(Continued)***

```
    public void PrinResults() {
      RowSet results = session.Execute("SELECT * FROM " +
        "portfolio_demo.portfolio WHERE portfolio_id = " +
        "756716f7-2e54-4715-9f00-91dcbea6cf50;");

      Console.WriteLine(String.Format("{0, -7}\t{1, -7}\t{2, -7}\t{3, -7}\r\n{4}",
        "Ticker", "Price", "Change", "PCT",
        "........+........+........+........"));

      foreach (Row row in results.GetRows()) {
        Console.WriteLine(String.Format("{0, -7}\t{1, -7}\t{2, -7}\t{3, -7}",
          row.GetValue@String:("ticker"),
          row.GetValue@Decimal:("current_price"),
          row.GetValue@Decimal:("current_change"),
          row.GetValue@float:("current_change_percent")));
      }
    }

    static void Main(string[] args) {
      SampleApp client = new SampleApp();
      client.Connect("127.0.0.1");
      client.CreateSchema();
      client.LoadData();
      client.PrinResults();
      client.Close();
    }
  }
}
```

Python

Though there are several Python drivers out there, the current driver that fully supports the CQL 3 Binary Protocol is the driver distributed by DataStax. To install the Python driver, ensure that you have pip already installed on your system and run `pip install cassandra-driver`.

To start the example, we will first create an empty class with a cluster and a session variable. We will also need to import our required package. Listing 9.15 outlines how to import the required packages and create our sample class.

Listing 9.15 **Creating a Sample Class in Python**

```
from cassandra.cluster import Cluster

class SampleApp(object):
  cluster = None
  session = None
```

Connecting

When connecting to the cluster, we need to specify only a single node. The driver will automatically query for information about the cluster and build a connection to each of the nodes in the cluster. Listing 9.16 shows how to connect to a cluster and print out information about the connections to the cluster.

Listing 9.16 **Using Python to Connect to a Cluster**

```
def connect(self, host):
  self.cluster = Cluster(host)
  self.session = self.cluster.connect()
  print "Cluster: %s" % self.cluster.metadata.cluster_name
  for host in self.cluster.metadata.all_hosts():
    print "Host: %s" % host
```

Disconnecting

To disconnect from the cluster, all you need to do is call `shutdown` on the cluster object. Listing 9.17 shows how to do this.

Listing 9.17 **Using Python to Disconnect from a Cluster**

```
def close(self):
  self.cluster.shutdown()
```

Schema Creation

Now that all of the connections have been created, we can create our schema. When creating the schema, we can use the optional `IF NOT EXISTS` conditional, which will allow running the command multiple times without error. When this conditional is not specified, additional executions of the schema creation code will result in an error. This conditional is available only in Cassandra 2.0 and later. Listing 9.18 shows how to create a keyspace and a sample table.

Listing 9.18 **Creating a Schema in Python**

```
def create_schema(self):
  self.session.execute("CREATE KEYSPACE IF NOT EXISTS portfolio_demo "
                       "WITH REPLICATION = { 'class': 'SimpleStrategy', "
                       "'replication_factor': 1 };")

  self.session.execute("CREATE TABLE IF NOT EXISTS "
                       "portfolio_demo.portfolio (portfolio_id UUID, "
                       "ticker TEXT, current_price DECIMAL, "
                       "current_change DECIMAL, "
                       "current_change_percent FLOAT, "
                       "PRIMARY KEY(portfolio_id, ticker));")
```

Writing Data

Once our schema has been created, we can load in some data. In this example, we will add a couple of rows to our table. Listing 9.19 shows example insert statements.

Listing 9.19 **Writing Data in Python**

```
def load_data(self):
  self.session.execute("INSERT INTO portfolio_demo.portfolio "
                       "(portfolio_id, ticker, current_price, "
                       " current_change, current_change_percent) VALUES "
                       "(756716f7-2e54-4715-9f00-91dcbea6cf50, 'GOOG', "
                       " 889.07, -4.00, -0.45);")

  self.session.execute("INSERT INTO portfolio_demo.portfolio "
                       "(portfolio_id, ticker, current_price, "
                       " current_change, current_change_percent) VALUES "
                       "(756716f7-2e54-4715-9f00-91dcbea6cf50, 'AMZN', "
                       " 297.92, -0.94, -0.31);")
```

Reading Data

When reading data, the query execution will return an iterable set of results that will allow access to the values of the fields requested. Listing 9.20 shows query execution and printing the results to the console.

Listing 9.20 **Reading Data in Python**

```
def print_results(self):
  results = self.session.execute("SELECT * FROM portfolio_demo.portfolio "
                                 "WHERE portfolio_id = "
                                 "756716f7-2e54-4715-9f00-91dcbea6cf50;")

  print "%-7s\t%-7s\t%-7s\t%-7s\n%s" % \
       ("Ticker", "Price", "Change", "PCT",
        "........+........+........+........")

  for row in results:
    print "%-7s\t%0.2f\t%0.2f\t%0.2f" % \
          (row.ticker, row.current_price, row.current_change,
          row.current_change_percent)
```

Putting It All Together

Listing 9.21 shows the entire sample class as it would look in an application.

Listing 9.21 **Full Python Sample**

```
from cassandra.cluster import Cluster
```

```
class SampleApp(object):

  cluster = None
  session = None

  def connect(self, host):
    self.cluster = Cluster(host)
    self.session = self.cluster.connect()
    print "Cluster: %s" % self.cluster.metadata.cluster_name
    for host in self.cluster.metadata.all_hosts():
      print "Host: %s" % host

  def close(self):
    self.cluster.shutdown()

  def create_schema(self):
    self.session.execute("CREATE KEYSPACE IF NOT EXISTS portfolio_demo "
                         "WITH REPLICATION = { 'class': 'SimpleStrategy', "
                         "'replication_factor': 1 };")

    self.session.execute("CREATE TABLE IF NOT EXISTS "
                         "portfolio_demo.portfolio (portfolio_id UUID, "
                         "ticker TEXT, current_price DECIMAL, "
                         "current_change DECIMAL, "
                         "current_change_percent FLOAT, "
                         "PRIMARY KEY(portfolio_id, ticker));")

  def load_data(self):
    self.session.execute("INSERT INTO portfolio_demo.portfolio "
                         "(portfolio_id, ticker, current_price, "
                         " current_change, current_change_percent) VALUES "
                         "(756716f7-2e54-4715-9f00-91dcbea6cf50, 'GOOG', "
                         " 889.07, -4.00, -0.45);")

    self.session.execute("INSERT INTO portfolio_demo.portfolio "
                         "(portfolio_id, ticker, current_price, "
                         " current_change, current_change_percent) VALUES "
                         "(756716f7-2e54-4715-9f00-91dcbea6cf50, 'AMZN', "
                         " 297.92, -0.94, -0.31);")

  def print_results(self):
    results = self.session.execute("SELECT * FROM portfolio_demo.portfolio "
                                   "WHERE portfolio_id = "
                                   "756716f7-2e54-4715-9f00-91dcbea6cf50;")
```

(Continues)

Listing 9.21 **Full Python Sample *(Continued)***

```
    print "%-7s\t%-7s\t%-7s\t%-7s\n%s" % \
          ("Ticker", "Price", "Change", "PCT",
           "........+........+........+........")

    for row in results:
      print "%-7s\t%0.2f\t%0.2f\t%0.2f" % \
            (row.ticker, row.current_price, row.current_change,
             row.current_change_percent)

if __name__ == '__main__':
  sample_app = SampleApp()
  sample_app.connect("127.0.0.1")
  sample_app.create_schema()
  sample_app.load_data()
  sample_app.print_results()
  sample_app.close()
```

Ruby

Theo Hultberg currently, as of this writing, maintains the most up-to-date Ruby driver for Cassandra. CQL-RB supports almost all functions in the CQL 3 spec and is consistently adding new features. As with the DataStax drivers, CQL-RB supports host detection as well as connecting to nodes that have failed. To install CQL-RB, simply run `gem install cql-rb` or add `cql-rb` to your Gemfile.

To start the example, we will first create an empty class with a cluster `attr_accessor`. We will also need to require the `cql` package. Listing 9.22 outlines how to import the required packages and create our sample class.

Listing 9.22 **Creating a Sample Class in Ruby**

```
require 'cql'

class SampleApp

end
```

Connecting

When connecting to the cluster, we need to specify only a single node. The driver will automatically query for information about the cluster and build a connection to each of the nodes in the cluster. Listing 9.23 shows how to connect to a cluster and print out information about the connections to the cluster.

Listing 9.23 **Using Ruby to Connect to a Cluster**

```
def connect host
  @cluster = Cql::Client.connect(host: host)
  puts 'Connected'
end
```

Disconnecting

To disconnect from the cluster, all you need to do is call `close` on the cluster object. Listing 9.24 shows how to do this.

Listing 9.24 **Using Ruby to Disconnect from a Cluster**

```
def close
 @cluster.close
end
```

Schema Creation

Now that all of the connections have been created, we can create our schema. When creating the schema, we can use the optional `IF NOT EXISTS` conditional, which will allow running the command multiple times without error. When this conditional is not specified, additional executions of the schema creation code will result in an error. This conditional is available only in Cassandra 2.0 and later. Listing 9.25 shows how to create a keyspace and a sample table.

Listing 9.25 **Creating a Schema in Ruby**

```
def create_schema
 create_keyspace = <<-CQL
  CREATE KEYSPACE IF NOT EXISTS portfolio_demo
    WITH REPLICATION = { 'class': 'SimpleStrategy',
                         'replication_factor': 1 };
 CQL

 create_portfolio = <<-CQL
  CREATE TABLE IF NOT EXISTS portfolio_demo.portfolio (
   portfolio_id UUID,
   ticker TEXT,
   current_price DECIMAL,
   current_change DECIMAL,
   current_change_percent FLOAT,
   PRIMARY KEY(portfolio_id, ticker)
  );
 CQL

 @cluster.execute(create_keyspace)
 @cluster.execute(create_portfolio)
end
```

Writing Data

Once our schema has been created, we can load in some data. In this example, we will add a couple of rows to our table. Listing 9.26 shows example insert statements.

Listing 9.26 **Writing Data in Ruby**

```
def load_data
  row_one = <<-CQL
    INSERT INTO portfolio_demo.portfolio
      (portfolio_id, ticker, current_price,
       current_change, current_change_percent)
    VALUES
      (756716f7-2e54-4715-9f00-91dcbea6cf50,
       'GOOG', 889.07, -4.00, -0.45);
  CQL

  row_two = <<-CQL
    INSERT INTO portfolio_demo.portfolio
      (portfolio_id, ticker, current_price,
       current_change, current_change_percent)
    VALUES
      (756716f7-2e54-4715-9f00-91dcbea6cf50,
       'AMZN', 297.92, -0.94, -0.31);
  CQL

  @cluster.execute(row_one)
  @cluster.execute(row_two)
end
```

Reading Data

When reading data, the query execution will return an iterable set of results that will allow access to the values of the fields requested. Listing 9.27 shows query execution and printing the results to the console.

Listing 9.27 **Reading Data in Ruby**

```
def print_results
  fields = %w(ticker current_price current_change current_change_percent)
  results_query = <<-CQL
    SELECT * FROM portfolio_demo.portfolio
      WHERE portfolio_id = 756716f7-2e54-4715-9f00-91dcbea6cf50;
  CQL
  puts "Ticker\tPrice\tChange\tPCT"
  puts '........+........+........+........'

  results = @cluster.execute(results_query)
  results.each do |row|
    puts "%s\t%0.2f\t%0.2f\t%0.2f" % fields.map{|f| row[f] }
  end
end
```

Putting It All Together

Listing 9.28 shows the entire sample class as it would look in an application.

Listing 9.28 **Full Ruby Example**

```
require 'cql'

class SampleApp

 def connect host
  @cluster = Cql::Client.connect(host: host)
 end

 def close
  @cluster.close
 end

 def create_schema
  create_keyspace = <<-CQL
   CREATE KEYSPACE IF NOT EXISTS portfolio_demo
     WITH REPLICATION = { 'class': 'SimpleStrategy',
                          'replication_factor': 1 };
  CQL

  create_portfolio = <<-CQL
   CREATE TABLE IF NOT EXISTS portfolio_demo.portfolio (
    portfolio_id UUID,
    ticker TEXT,
    current_price DECIMAL,
    current_change DECIMAL,
    current_change_percent FLOAT,
    PRIMARY KEY(portfolio_id, ticker)
   );
  CQL

  @cluster.execute(create_keyspace)
  @cluster.execute(create_portfolio)
 end

 def load_data
  row_one = <<-CQL
   INSERT INTO portfolio_demo.portfolio
     (portfolio_id, ticker, current_price,
      current_change, current_change_percent)
   VALUES
     (756716f7-2e54-4715-9f00-91dcbea6cf50,
      'GOOG', 889.07, -4.00, -0.45);
  CQL
```

(Continues)

Listing 9.28 **Full Ruby Example *(Continued)***

```
  row_two = <<-CQL
   INSERT INTO portfolio_demo.portfolio
     (portfolio_id, ticker, current_price,
      current_change, current_change_percent)
   VALUES
     (756716f7-2e54-4715-9f00-91dcbea6cf50,
      'AMZN', 297.92, -0.94, -0.31);
  CQL

  @cluster.execute(row_one)
  @cluster.execute(row_two)
 end

 def print_results
  fields = %w(ticker current_price current_change current_change_percent)
  results_query = <<-CQL
   SELECT * FROM portfolio_demo.portfolio
    WHERE portfolio_id = 756716f7-2e54-4715-9f00-91dcbea6cf50;
  CQL

  puts "Ticker\tPrice\tChange\tPCT"
  puts '........+........+........+........'

  results = @cluster.execute(results_query)
  results.each do |row|
   puts "%s\t%0.2f\t%0.2f\t%0.2f" % fields.map{|f| row[f] }
  end
 end

end

if __FILE__ == $0
 sample_app = SampleApp.new
 sample_app.connect '127.0.0.1'
 sample_app.create_schema
 sample_app.load_data
 sample_app.print_results
 sample_app.close
end
```

Summary

In this chapter, we demonstrated how to create a simple application in four of the most commonly used languages. The demonstrations showed how to connect to a cluster, create a schema, load and read data, and finally disconnect from the cluster. The sample application and code will be available on GitHub at https://github.com/devdazed/cassandra-sample-application. For more information on Cassandra, drivers, tutorials, and training, you can visit http://planetcassandra.org.

10

Troubleshooting

Knowing a little about how a system works is one of the keys to troubleshooting it. In this chapter, we will discuss some of the ways to troubleshoot Cassandra and the tools involved.

Toolkit

Most of the tools that are used for troubleshooting are basic *nix tools. We'll go over some of the key command-line switches and what to look for when examining a system.

iostat

iostat is a commonly used *nix tool that shows metrics about the input/output of a system. It does not come installed out of the box on most *nix distributions. It is commonly found as part of the `sysstat` package. The following is taken from the `iostat` man page that comes with Linux:

> The `iostat` command is used for monitoring system input/output device loading by observing the time the devices are active in relation to their average transfer rates.

One of the common first signs that your cluster is having I/O troubles is the await (average wait) time. Average wait time (measured by `iostat` in milliseconds) is the length of time for I/O requests issued to a device to be served. This includes the time spent by the requests in queue and the time spent servicing them. Listing 10.1 shows what a normal but active system's device average wait time for I/O looks like via `iostat`.

Listing 10.1 **Normal** `iostat`

```
# iostat -dx 2
Device:    rrqm/s    wrqm/s      r/s     w/s    rsec/s    wsec/s    avgrq-sz    avgqu-sz
xvdb         0.00      0.00    12.50    1.60    362.10    114.20       33.16        0.11
await       svctm     %util
9.78         4.97      5.65

Device:    rrqm/s    wrqm/s      r/s     w/s    rsec/s    wsec/s    avgrq-sz    avgqu-sz
xvdb         0.00      0.00    10.00    1.20    340.80    102.40       39.57        0.10
await       svctm     %util
9.29         4.82      5.40
```

What an average wait time means is that each time an application wants to read from the disk, this is the number of milliseconds that the request takes (on average) to be served up to an application. In other words, "How long does my database have to wait to get information off the disk?" This time includes time spent servicing the existing requests in the I/O wait queue. The higher the average I/O wait time number gets, the worse state your system is in.

So let's compare the output of `iostat` shown in Listing 10.2 on an overly active system for the same device. It is easy to see that the average wait time is really high. For this machine, the average time Cassandra has to wait when it has a request that requires the disk to be serviced is approximately three seconds. The `-d` switch is telling `iostat` to show only the device-level information. The `-x` switch is telling `iostat` to show extended stats. The `2` is telling `iostat` to print the stats to the screen every two seconds.

Listing 10.2 **Very Active Device `iostat` Output**

```
# iostat -dx 2
Device:    rrqm/s   wrqm/s     r/s     w/s   rsec/s   wsec/s   avgrq-sz   avgqu-sz
xvdb        74.20    46.80  672.30    1.45 25241.30   131.80      69.60      92.71
await      svctm    %util
3124.12     2.36    91.00

Device:    rrqm/s   wrqm/s     r/s     w/s   rsec/s   wsec/s   avgrq-sz   avgqu-sz
xvdb        73.40    44.50  667.20    1.40 24753.60   122.40      67.40      92.58
await      svctm    %util
2976.68     2.39    88.00
```

Again, it is important to note that `iostat` is an indicator of a potential problem, not an absolute. So take the results of analyzing the output of `iostat` into account when looking into issues, but don't use them as an absolute measure of a problem. One of the primary assumptions being made when asking the question "How much time does it take Cassandra to read from the disk?" is that Cassandra is the primary application on the machine competing for disk access.

`dstat`

dstat is another excellent tool for seeing the overall health of your system. Like `iostat`, `dstat` does not come installed with most common operating systems.

Listing 10.3 shows an example of `dstat` output on a healthy active Cassandra cluster. There are a few switches that are handy to be aware of. The `-l` switch tells `dstat` to print the system load information. The `-n` switch tells `dstat` to print the network information. The `-v` switch tells `dstat` to show the output in a `vmstat` style (`vmstat` is short for Virtual Memory Statistics, which is another *nix tool). The `-r` switch tells `dstat` to show I/O request information. The `10` tells `dstat` to show a new line once every ten seconds.

Listing 10.3 **Example Output of `dstat` on a Healthy Active Cassandra Cluster**

```
# dstat -lnvr 10
...load-avg... -net/total- ...procs... ......memory-usage..... -paging-
 1m   5m  15m| recv send|run blk new|     used buff cach free| in   out |
1.15 1.34 1.57|    0    0 |  0 0.0 1.8|10.3G 3164k 4421M 71.5M|  0    0 |
1.35 1.38 1.58|1197k 863k|2.0 1.6 0.4|10.3G 3172k 4417M 75.1M|  0    0 |
1.22 1.35 1.57|1230k 936k|1.1 1.0 1.9|10.3G 3172k 4422M 70.8M|  0    0 |
1.42 1.39 1.58|1188k 914k|1.3 1.3 4.1|10.3G 3172k 4416M 76.6M|  0    0 |
-dsk/total- ---system-- ----total-cpu-usage------ -io/total-
 read writ| int   csw|usr sys idl wai hiq siq| read writ
3193k 642k|1761   13k| 18   6  70   6   0   1|  142 15.7
4175k 530k| 11k  9771| 12   4  64  19   0   0|  239 12.7
3820k 524k| 12k   12k| 11   3  69  16   0   1|  213 12.6
4440k 766k| 11k  9799| 11   3  68  17   0   0|  223 19.3
```

As with any introspection tool, it is necessary to know what your system looks like when it is performing normally in order to see where there could be potential problems. Using a tool such as `dstat` will enable you to see how Cassandra is interacting with the disk, memory, CPU, and network. If there are any bottlenecks, they should be easy to see.

One of the easiest ways to see the onset of a problem is just to watch the system load average. The system load average is a gauge of how many processes are, on average, concurrently demanding CPU attention. As a general rule, you should divide the load average by the number of CPUs for multicore systems. The system load itself will usually not be helpful in determining what a problem is, but watching it regularly should help to establish a pattern of normal system behavior. Running `dstat` and having a new line print every ten minutes is a good way to see how your system reacts to the various points of an hour or day. If you start to see the load average spike, it's time to start investigating further.

`nodetool`

Many of the troubleshooting mechanisms that involve `nodetool` were covered in previous chapters. But it is important to keep in mind that the output of some of the `nodetool` commands is usually the insight you need to investigate issues with nodes and ultimately the cluster. The most common `nodetool` commands for checking the health of a node within your cluster are `cfstats`, `tpstats`, `info`, `netstats`, and `compactionstats`.

Common Problems

Some common Cassandra problems already have well-defined solutions that you can try. Here, we have included some of the more common problems that are seen by Cassandra users as well as some of the possible solutions. Your mileage may vary.

Slow Reads, Fast Writes

One of the most common problems of a schema that is not properly set up is that you start to see your reads slowing down and your write speeds staying consistent (or at least not slowing down in comparison to the reads). Listing 10.4 shows an example of `cfstats` output with high read latency.

Listing 10.4 `cfstats` **Output with a High Read Latency**

```
# nodetool cfstats | grep -A 19 events_2013_06
              Column Family: events_2013_06
              SSTable count: 4
              Space used (live): 26422246080
              Space used (total): 26422246080
              Number of Keys (estimate): 11566336
              Memtable Columns Count: 46240
              Memtable Data Size: 79644540
              Memtable Switch Count: 1116
              Read Count: 7867823
              Read Latency: 185.175 ms.
              Write Count: 170267477
              Write Latency: 0.025 ms.
              Pending Tasks: 3
              Bloom Filter False Positives: 0
              Bloom Filter False Ratio: 0.00000
              Bloom Filter Space Used: 25018624
              Compacted row minimum size: 373
              Compacted row maximum size: 962624926
              Compacted row mean size: 18170
```

There are a number of ways to see that the read capacity of your system isn't keeping up. The first is to use `nodetool cfstats` to see how many SSTables are in the ColumnFamily. If that number is continually increasing, your cluster's I/O capacity isn't high enough to keep up with the write load. And because the compactions aren't taking place (quickly enough) to group the necessary data together properly in the SSTables, the data is getting fragmented across the SSTables. The way to fix this is by adding more I/O capacity. This can be done by either increasing the disk speed (with something like SSDs) or increasing the number of nodes in the cluster.

On the other hand, if the SSTable count is low, take a look at the file cache on each machine as it compares to the read pattern. To calculate the amount of file cache, you can use the formula of total_system_memory – JVM_heap_size. If the amount of data is greater than that, and you have a roughly random read pattern, then an equal ratio of reads to the cache-to-data ratio will need to seek to the disk. In other words, you may be able to deal with some of the read issues by enabling key or row caches (by setting `KEYS_ONLY`, `ROWS_ONLY`, or `ALL`). It is also worth noting that if you set the cache to use row caching, ensure that the row cache stays relatively small (about 20,000 rows); the key cache can be at 100%.

Freezing Nodes

You may run into a situation where the operating system is still responding normally, but Cassandra seems to be moving slowly. The first thing to check is whether garbage collection is running. In your Cassandra system.log you should look for entries that reference GCInspector, indicating that either ParNew or the ConcurrentMarkSweep collectors are taking a long time to run. You will likely see entries that look somewhat similar to Listing 10.5. These are entries pulled from a machine that is having GC issues. Notice that the total time spent in GC is high (ranging from a few seconds up to a few minutes).

Listing 10.5 **Example Log Entries for Long-Running GCs**

```
INFO [ScheduledTasks:1] 2013-02-20 15:40:57,096 GCInspector.java (line 122) GC for
ParNew: 17305 ms for 1 collections, 2634113808 used; max is 7432306688
INFO [GC inspection] 2013-02-20 15:49:45,973 GCInspector.java (line 116) GC for
ConcurrentMarkSweep: 775679 ms, 745236442 reclaimed leaving 13692736 used; max is
7432306688
INFO [ScheduledTasks:1] 2013-02-20 16:20:45,800 GCInspector.java (line 122) GC for
ParNew: 11080 ms for 2 collections, 885296848 used; max is 7432306688
INFO [GC inspection] 2013-02-20 16:26:41,136 GCInspector.java (line 116) GC for
ConcurrentMarkSweep: 135562 ms, 814236544 reclaimed leaving 20652193 used; max is
7432306688
INFO [ScheduledTasks:1] 2013-02-20 17:29:27,148 GCInspector.java (line 122) GC for
ParNew: 16204 ms for 1 collections, 4259366008 used; max is 7432306688
```

GC should not take longer than a few hundred milliseconds to run on a normally functioning cluster. In some edge cases of a normally functioning cluster, you may see your GC patterns moving up to ten to 15 seconds. GC that frequently takes more than 15 seconds requires some investigation. The most likely cause is that some portion of the JVM is being swapped out of memory by the OS. A common problem is that memory-mapped DiskAccessMode is being used without JNA (Java Native Access) support. The address space will eventually be exhausted by the memory map, and the OS will swap out the portion of the memory that isn't in use. The JVM will eventually try to GC this space to reclaim it (which will take a while).

When this happens, there are a few solutions that can be implemented. Adding the JNA libraries to the Cassandra class path is the first possibility. They can't be shipped with Cassandra because of the GPL licensing on the JNA libraries, but they are freely available for download. The JNA libraries can be downloaded from GitHub (https://github.com/twall/jna). The other option is to set the DiskAccessMode to `mmap_index_only`. This will ensure that Cassandra memory-maps only the indexes and will therefore use much less memory address space.

It is generally recommended that you shut off swapping if the machine is running only Cassandra. This lets the OS out-of-memory (OOM) killer kill the Java process rather than letting it swap for a while before it eventually runs out of memory itself. Along this same line, if the GCInspector isn't reporting excessively long GC times but the GC times are regularly taking longer, it may be that the JVM is dealing with heavy GC pressure and will eventually run out of memory.

Tracking Down OOM Errors

OOM errors are not uncommon in Java, and there are definitely ways of dealing with them. This is true for Cassandra as well. The following sections present a few common reasons that Cassandra will die for OOM reasons and what can be done about them.

Caching Is Too Large

This is commonly attributed to the row cache being too large but can be a function of either the key cache or the row cache. If your ColumnFamily cache settings are either `ROWS_ONLY` or `ALL`, you can remove at least the row cache and drop it down to key caching (by using `KEYS_ONLY` as the cache setting in the ColumnFamily). Since caching rows is a high-end optimization, it is likely that Cassandra can run very well without it.

If you don't want to change the caching levels on each ColumnFamily specifically, you can also change the configuration at a higher level, in the cassandra.yaml file. The two main settings to adjust are the `key_cache_size_in_mb` and the `row_cache_size_in_mb`. By making these two values smaller, you may be able to prevent the OOM issues.

It is also possible that you may not be using your caches efficiently. The default `row_cache_provider` is the SerializingCacheProvider. It is the most memory efficient and for non-blob-intensive applications is only about a five to ten times increase in the amount of memory used. The other option, if you have a more update-heavy workload, is to use the ConcurrentLinkedHashCacheProvider. Unlike the SerializingCacheProvider, which updates rows in place on change, the ConcurrentLinkedHashCacheProvider just invalidates cached rows in memory on change. Ideally, you want to see about a 90% hit rate for row caches. If you can't get to that, you should likely switch the cache to `KEYS_ONLY` to preserve the extra cache space for other ColumnFamilys.

MemTable Sizes Are Too Large for the JVM Heap

Cassandra generally puts $n + 2$ MemTables into resident memory where n is the number of ColumnFamilys in the keyspace. Add another 1GB on top of that for Cassandra to determine the best total heap size. However, going much beyond 8GB for the heap is not generally a good idea to begin with. The more memory used in the heap, the longer the GC pause will be. A GC pause means that nearly everything else in the system is put on hold until the garbage collection has completed.

Ring View Differs between Nodes

When the ring view differs between nodes, it is never a good thing. There is also no easy way to recover from this state. The only way to recover is to do a full cluster restart. A rolling restart won't work because the Gossip protocol from the bad nodes will inform the newly booting good nodes of the bad state. A full cluster restart and bringing the good nodes up first should enable the cluster to come back up in a good state.

Insufficient User Resources

Any insufficient resource errors that appear in the logs may not initially appear to be caused by insufficient resources. In other words, the errors are not as explicit as just say-ing the resources are insufficient. Here are some of the log lines that you may see and their associated error type:

- Insufficient as (address space) or `memlock` setting:
  `ERROR [SSTableBatchOpen:1] 2012-07-25 15:46:02,913 AbstractCassandraDaemon.java (line 139) Fatal exception in thread Thread[SSTableBatchOpen:1,5,main] java.io.IOError: java.io.IOException: Map failed at . . .`
- Insufficient `memlock` settings:
  `WARN [main] 2011-06-15 09:58:56,861 CLibrary.java (line 118) Unable to lock JVM memory (ENOMEM)`
  This can result in part of the JVM being swapped out, especially with memory-mapped I/O enabled. Increase `RLIMIT_MEMLOCK` or run Cassandra as root.
- Insufficient `nofiles` setting (example 1):
  `WARN 05:13:43,644 Transport error occurred during acceptance of message.`
  `org.apache.thrift.transport.TTransportException: java.net.SocketException:`
  `Too many open files . . .`
- Insufficient `nofiles` setting (example 2):
  `ERROR [MutationStage:11] 2012-04-30 09:46:08,102 AbstractCassandraDaemon.java (line 139) Fatal exception in thread Thread[MutationStage:11,5,main] java.lang.OutOfMemoryError: unable to create new native thread`

You can view the current limits using the `ulimit -a` command. Although limits can also be temporarily set using this command, it is recommended that you permanently change the settings by adding the entries shown in Listing 10.6 to your /etc/security/limits.conf file.

Listing 10.6 **limits.conf File Example for Cassandra Running as Root**

```
* soft nofile 32768
* hard nofile 32768
root soft nofile 32768
root hard nofile 32768
* soft memlock unlimited
* hard memlock unlimited
root soft memlock unlimited
root hard memlock unlimited
* soft as unlimited
* hard as unlimited
root soft as unlimited
root hard as unlimited
* soft nproc 10240    # CentOS/Red Hat systems
```

On CentOS or RedHat systems, change the system limits from 1024 to 10240 in /etc/security/limits.d/90-nproc.conf.

You also may need to run the `sysctl` command as shown in Listing 10.7 to change the `max_map_count` for the system. This is the maximum number of memory map areas that a process may have. The default value for this field is 65536. Most applications won't use anything even close to this value. Depending on your use case, Cassandra may use a lot more areas of memory than most applications. Doubling the default value should give you plenty of headroom.

Listing 10.7 `sysctl` **Update for** `max_map_count`

```
# sysctl -w vm.max_map_count = 131072
```

Summary

As with any complex system, there is a steep learning curve for understanding the behavior of your Cassandra cluster. It is not sufficient to figure out how your system performs under normal circumstances; you also need to know how it performs under load. Using some or all of the tools and techniques covered in this chapter will help you find and diagnose some of the more common issues when administering a Cassandra cluster.

11

Architecture

There are many components of Cassandra's architecture. This chapter provides an overview of some of the major pieces.

Meta Keyspaces

There are a few meta keyspaces in Cassandra. The System Keyspace is the most common one and the one that exists on all systems. There are special keyspaces within Cassandra that are used to store metadata about the cluster, users and authentication, and the other keyspaces. In the MySQL world, this would be the `mysql` database. In Mongo, this would be the `admin` database. In Oracle, this would be the `SYSTEM` tablespace. An example of another meta keyspace is the CFS (Cassandra File System) keyspace that is used (among other things) as an abstraction layer between a Hadoop connector and Cassandra so that Cassandra can properly provide Hadoop with the information it needs in the format it needs to process the data correctly.

The following section focuses on the aforementioned System Keyspace.

System Keyspace

Regardless of the placement strategy used in the cluster or ring as a whole, the System Keyspace is stored using LocalStrategy. The reason for this is that it contains the local node's view of the ring and therefore should not be replicated elsewhere.

Cassandra stores a few things in the System Keyspace. There are a few ColumnFamilys in the System Keyspace that keep track of information that is specific to the local node. The node-specific types of information are things like LocationInfo (or where the node sits in the ring in comparison to other nodes). The Hints ColumnFamily, stored in the System Keyspace, keeps track of Hints that have been created about writes for this node or received Hints from other nodes. This is one of the ways that data from around the ring stays in sync.

Information about all keyspaces is stored in the System Keyspace. The IndexInfo ColumnFamily keeps track of the indexes that have been created on the cluster. Index information stored in the IndexInfo ColumnFamily is for all indexes stored in all keyspaces. The Migrations ColumnFamily stores all information about schema migrations that take place. Schema migrations are when you change the schema in some way. These typically happen around ColumnFamily operations (create, update, and delete), but schemas also get updated when anything in the keyspace changes. The actual information that pertains specifically to the schema and its validation criteria is stored in `schema_columnfamilies`, `schema_columns`, and `schema_keyspaces`.

The Versions ColumnFamily shows you what versions of each of the primary systems you are using. This is typically things like the Cassandra version, Thrift version, and CQL version.

The System Keyspace is not something that should be modified by hand. While it can be changed, be very careful if you do so as some changes could create problems. It can be very difficult to recover from data corruption.

Authentication

Out of the box, Cassandra provides the capability to build your own authentication and authorization layers. Most people don't do that, nor do they have the need to do that, but setting up simple authentication and authorization is pretty straightforward. The default Cassandra setting for authentication is AllowAllAuthenticator, which is equivalent to no authentication. Setting this SimpleAuthenticator will enable the use of two files, the access.properties file and the password.properties file. If there are users specified in the access.properties file that don't have corresponding entries in the password file, they will not have access to Cassandra.

To use the access.properties file, all entries should be in the format shown in Listing 11.1. The first line of each file in the example is commented out for reference.

Listing 11.1 **Format of the access.properties File**

```
# $keyspace.$table.$permission=$user_list
video_store.videos.@rw:=randalgraves
```

To use the password.properties file, all entries should be in the format shown in Listing 11.2.

Listing 11.2 **Format of the password.properties File**

```
# $user=$password
randalgraves=videostoreclerk
```

Note that all passwords are stored in plaintext unless the `passwd.mode=MD5` is specified.

For example, say we want to control access to the VideoStore keyspace. Let's give `allclerks` read-only access, give `randalgraves` full read-write access, and give `dantehicks` read-only access to just the videos table. We need to first create the entries in the password file (see Listing 11.3).

Listing 11.3 **Example password.properties File**

```
dantehicks=hereondayoff
randalgraves=videostoreclerk
allclerks=lazy
```

Once the password entries have been created, it's time to add the access control. The file should look like Listing 11.4.

Listing 11.4 **Example access.properties File**

```
VideoStore.@ro:=allclerks
VideoStore.@rw:=randalgraves
VideoStore.videos.@ro:=dantehicks
```

Access control granularity works only down to the table level as of Cassandra 1.2 without custom access control. At a less granular level, you can give a user (in this case, the user's name is admin) the ability to modify everything within a keyspace by adding the line in Listing 11.5 to the access.properties file.

Listing 11.5 **Allow `videoadmin` User to Modify Anything within a Keyspace**

```
 # videoadmin can modify everything
<modify-keyspaces>=videoadmin
```

Gossip Protocol

The way that Cassandra nodes talk to each other is through something called the Gossip protocol. Using the Gossip protocol, each node has the ability to tell other nodes how it's doing and find out what other nodes are up to. In other words, the Gossip protocol exists to ensure that each node knows the state of itself and every other node in the ring.

The Gossip protocol works by creating a Gossiper endpoint when the system starts. This happens in the following manner:

1. When Cassandra starts up, it registers itself with the Gossiper to receive endpoint state information.
2. Periodically, typically once per second, the Gossiper will choose a random node in the ring and start a Gossip session with it. Each round of Gossip requires a set of three messages similar to a TCP transaction.
3. The node that is initiating the Gossip sends the receiving node a GossipDigestSynMessage. This means that it is requesting a synchronization.
4. When the receiving node gets the request, it will respond (assuming it's not dead) with a GossipDigestAckMessage. This means that the receiving node acknowledges the message.

5. Then the initiating node receives the ack message and it sends the receiving node a GossipDigestAck2Message.

Failure Detection

Gossip in the cluster happens frequently because the Gossip protocol is also responsible for failure detection of nodes. If the receiving node doesn't answer in a timely manner (or at all), the initiating node will assume that the node is down and mark it so within the ring information.

Failure of a node or group of nodes within a ring is handled by the Phi Accrual Failure Detection algorithm. As a result, the associated failure detection threshold setting is called the `*phi_convict_threshold*`. The Phi convict threshold is a setting that adjusts the sensitivity level of failure detection. It is worth noting that this setting is on an exponential scale. A lower value increases the likelihood that an unresponsive node will be marked as down. A higher value decreases the likelihood that a transient failure (such as temporary loss of network connectivity) will cause a node failure. The default setting is 8. If you are operating your infrastructure in the cloud or across data centers, you will want to give yourself a little room for failure and up the setting to 10 or 11.

CommitLogs and MemTables

All write operations in Cassandra first go through the CommitLog. It is mainly because of the CommitLog that Cassandra can attain such high write performance results. The CommitLog is so integral to a Cassandra mutation operation that an operation is not considered successful unless it has been written to the CommitLog. A mutation is any `INSERT`, `UPDATE`, or `DELETE` operation. The reason Cassandra is so fast about receiving the writes is that all operations are appended to the CommitLog sequentially. Sequential writes mean there are no disk seeks, and therefore the entire operation is much faster.

The order for a mutation operation is as follows. First, the operation comes in over the wire (possibly via CQL, Thrift, or any other means by which you communicate with Cassandra) and is written to the CommitLog. Once the operation has been written to disk and has satisfied the data durability requirements (in other words, this information is now recoverable), it is written to a MemTable. A MemTable is an in-memory key/value data structure similar to a cache. Each ColumnFamily has a separate MemTable. MemTables are flushed to disk when the number of keys in the MemTable exceed a predefined limit (128 keys is the default) or when the size of the allocated space for MemTables is exceeded.

SSTables

An SSTable is the way that Cassandra stores data on disk. Each SSTable is made up of five files: a bloom filter file, an index file, a compression file (optional) if the ColumnFamily data is compressed, a statistics file, and a data file. When each MemTable is flushed to disk, the following steps are gone through. First, the index needs to be written. In order to write the index, the columns are sorted by their row keys. Then the columns are iterated over and the bloom filter is created. Indexing is done based on the ColumnFamily comparator. Then the data is serialized and written to disk. The data file is written based on the partitioner, hashing algorithm, and compression options. If the data file is written as compressed, the CompressionInfo file is also written. After the other files have been written to disk, a ColumnFamilyStatistics file is written. This includes information such as the number of keys, row and column counts, and data sizes, to name a few items.

HintedHandoffs

Although HintedHandoffs are not required, they are highly encouraged. They serve two main purposes:

- They allow full write availability when consistency is not required. In other words, when the write consistency level is not set to `QUORUM`, `LOCAL_QUORUM`, or `ALL`, the HintedHandoff will ensure that the data gets to the other nodes.
- They improve response consistency after downtime such as network failures or power failures.

The way Hints work is that when a write request comes in and its destination is down or not responding, the coordinating node will store it locally. There is a ColumnFamily called Hints in the System Keyspace designed specifically for dealing with Hints. Similar to the Oplog in Mongo or Binlog in MySQL, the Hints table will enable another node to replay write operations the way they came in.

Once the coordinator node holding the Hints finds out that the downed node is back up, it will begin to send the rows corresponding to that node from the Hints table. The coordinator node will also check every ten minutes to see if there are any Hints for writes that timed out during an outage too brief for the FailureDetector to notice over the Gossip protocol.

There are a few items to be aware of with regard to HintedHandoffs. Hinted writes do not count toward ConsistencyLevel requirements. This means that a degraded cluster (a cluster that is missing one or more nodes) is still doing the same number of writes, just with fewer nodes to absorb the write load. Cassandra also attempts to be smart about Hints by doing things like removing Hints for nodes that have been decommissioned or had their tokens removed. It will also remove Hints for ColumnFamilys that have been dropped. The last item of note for HintedHandoffs is that they do not replace a repair on hardware failure. Historical data can be lost or Hints that have not been replayed on the downed node can potentially show up as missing data. As a result, repairs after a hardware failure or extended outage period are advised.

Bloom Filters

A bloom filter is a space-efficient probabilistic data structure that is used to determine whether or not an element is a member of a set. False positives are possible. False negatives are not. A false positive means that the data structure thinks the value is on the node when it actually is not. A false negative is when the bloom filter thinks the data is not on a node when it actually is.

The reason that bloom filters are used in Cassandra is to determine whether an SSTable has data for a particular row. They are used for index scans, but not for range scans. On a per-ColumnFamily basis, the higher the `bloom_filter_fp_chance` setting, the less memory will be used. However, this will result in greater disk I/O as the SSTables get more highly fragmented.

It is important to note that starting in Cassandra version 1.2, bloom filters are no longer stored on-heap. This means that they don't need to be taken into consideration when determining the maximum memory sizes for the JVM.

Compaction Types

Initially, all data passed into Cassandra hits the disk via the CommitLog. Once the CommitLog segment is complete, it gets rolled up (or compacted) into separate SSTables. There are two common strategies for this compaction. There is the default type of size-tiered or the less commonly used type of leveled.

SizeTieredCompaction

The default type of compaction on Cassandra, SizeTieredCompaction, is made for insert-heavy workloads that are lighter on the reads. The key issue with SizeTieredCompaction is that it requires at least twice the available size on disk in order to be used properly. In other words, if you have 400GB of data in your SSTables on a 500GB drive, you will likely not be able to complete a compaction. Compactions can take up to two times the size of the data on disk in the worst of scenarios. The size of the SSTables being compacted is what determines how much available disk space is required for the compaction.

LeveledCompaction

The LeveledCompactionStrategy is based on Google's LevelDB. It is best suited for ColumnFamilys with read-heavy workloads that have frequent updates to existing rows (as opposed to frequent creation of new rows). If you use LeveledCompaction, you will want to keep an eye on the read latency for that ColumnFamily. If the nodes in the cluster can't keep up with the write workload and the number of pending compactions is rising, the read performance will begin to suffer even more. One of the major benefits of using LeveledCompaction is that you are not required to perform the major compactions as frequently as you do on the SizeTieredCompaction-based ColumnFamilys. Another major benefit is that you do not need to keep double the amount of data on disk available to perform these compactions when you do run them.

Tombstones

A tombstone is the special name for a value that marks a column as being deleted. In a distributed system, writes (and therefore deletes) are typically done under the assumption that not all nodes that contain the data need to be made aware of the operation (according to the client). So when a delete operation happens on some nodes and not others, Cassandra will mark the deleted row or column with a tombstone and pass this marking along to the other machines responsible for the same amount of data. Since data cannot be removed immediately, the tombstone is added to the CommitLog and the actual data is removed from the SSTable on the next compaction.

Cassandra has specifically designed a methodology for taking care of tombstones. There is a constant called GCGraceSeconds. Each node tracks the age of each tombstone locally. Once the tombstone has aged past that constant of GCGraceSeconds, it can be garbage collected during a compaction. This is to say that if a node is out of service for longer than GCGraceSeconds, you should treat that node as failed and replace it (typically re-bootstrapping works well). The typical setting for GCGraceSeconds is ten days. But this is something that should be tuned for your environment.

Staged Event-Driven Architecture

Cassandra was built with staged event-driven architecture (SEDA) as one of the core concurrency models. What this means is that instead of doing all work for a particular operation within a single thread, work begins in one thread and is then handed off to one or many other threads for the operation to complete. In other words, work is divided up into stages, and then thread pools are created for each stage. This enables Cassandra to manage its own resources internally and can then be optimized for whichever performance characteristic is best for the situation (I/O, CPU, memory, network, etc.).

As is typical of evented models, each stage is made up of an event handler, an event queue, and an associated thread pool for handling those events. Cassandra is extremely effective at using this model for concurrency as it can reallocate resources as necessary to keep up with the load being thrown at it. The most common stages in this architecture are

- Read
- Mutation
- Gossip
- Response
- Anti-entropy
- Load balance
- Migration
- Streaming

While there are some more granular subdivisions within these stages, Cassandra's workflow uses these at a high level. If any of these stages becomes overloaded with work, Cassandra can (and will) drop operations waiting in the event queue of the stage to keep the node available. This architecture is one of the ways that Cassandra keeps itself highly available.

Note

The original SEDA paper is available at www.eecs.harvard.edu/~mdw/proj/seda.

Summary

There are many facets to understanding how Cassandra processes data and manages its peers. Many of these complexities are intentionally abstracted from the user to ensure things work out of the box. There are many knobs that can be tuned to adjust for a particular use case, such as choosing a compaction type or setting the `bloom_filter_fp_chance` value for a ColumnFamily. Understanding how Cassandra works under the covers not only can help you troubleshoot problems but can also help you make decisions for your data, schema, and usage patterns for creating and scaling your system.

12
Case Studies

We have provided some case studies of various companies that are using Cassandra internally to give you a few ideas of the way other people think about Cassandra. Information will range from how Cassandra applications are built to how the deployments and data modeling are done.

Ooyala

Evan Chan and Al Tobey

At Ooyala, we deliver personalized video experiences across many types of platforms. We are a leader in online video management, publishing, analytics, and monetization. Our goal in analytics is to give content owners rich, actionable insights that increase their video engagement.

If you have watched a video on espn.com, you have probably used Ooyala technology.

The first pass at Ooyala's analytics was built on MySQL. It worked well for a while but quickly started to cause problems when MapReduce jobs hammered so many writes to the database that slave replication wasn't able to keep up. The database infrastructure couldn't take the abuse, and it was time to look for a new solution.

Before we decided to follow through with using Cassandra (which was only 0.4 at the time), we investigated a few other possibilities, including HBase and other NoSQL solutions. We ultimately decided on Cassandra.

Cassandra was chosen because it presents the BigTable data model that was familiar to many of our engineers. It also had a decent Ruby driver, which fit well into the development platform that was in place. The Cassandra user community was relatively active. Finally, Cassandra had no trouble taking a beating from our Hadoop cluster on writes.

We started using Cassandra for analytics aggregates, and the use cases multiplied. The analytics module in our video player reports playback information back to our analytics collection servers, and the data is written into log files. From there, the following takes place:

- Logs are aggregated into metrics via Hadoop and written into Cassandra.

- Other pipelines create trends and user/video clustering data that is also written to Cassandra.
- Cassandra is also used for real-time stream access and other real-time user management.

That all worked really well for quite a while. As we started to grow larger and larger as a company, we had to scale various parts of the solution at different rates. We would spin up single-use Cassandra clusters, and they would just hum along in the background with little to no management (which we don't recommend). Eventually, we realized that we had to bring all our concerns back together and build a modern analytics stack. We had success doing stream processing of our real-time data in Storm and realized we could use a similar system to write our data into Cassandra as it arrived.

For our next-generation analytics stack, we started by writing the over two billion raw video events per day (over 25,000 per second) into a big Cassandra cluster. They are written into a time-series wide row schema, which looks like what is shown in Listing 12.1.

Listing 12.1 **Raw Event Data and Event Attribute Data**

```
Event  CF:
 2013-08-26#++0Bo06:  2013-09-14T22:06:29.000Z: {"eventType":1, "lastEvent-
Time":1379196388}  2013-09-14T22:06:29.001Z: {"eventType":19,
"firstForPlayer":true}
EventAttr  CF: 2013-08-26#++0Bo06:  ipaddr:   174.89.195.19  region:   ontario
videoId:   21856838  providerId: 25322  countryCode: ca  device-type: Tablet
```

Storing user attributes into a separate ColumnFamily enables us to do easy filtering/indexing, as well as makes it possible to do post-ingestion update of attributes. It also saves a lot of space.

From here, the challenge is how we turn the mountain of raw events into small, actionable nuggets of truth. And how do we make the development and querying of these insights quick, scalable, and easy? Traditionally, real-time queries for Cassandra have involved minimizing the number of rows you have to read from.

Hadoop is very scalable but very slow, and the programming API lacks features. Also, the built-in Cassandra InputFormat is designed only for reading an entire ColumnFamily of data. Real-time streaming frameworks such as Storm are a good fit for fixed processing from firehoses but not so good for flexible queries from a data store. Thus, we have turned to Spark, a very fast, in-memory distributed computing framework, to help us with these insights.

Spark is used to run distributed jobs that read raw player events from Cassandra and generate materialized views, which are cached in memory. These materialized views can then be queried using subsequent jobs. Spark is fast enough that these jobs running on materialized views can be used for interactive queries!

An example materialized view would have country, region, device type, and other metrics as columns. Thus, finding out what the top device types in the United States are would involve a query like that shown in Listing 12.2. This query would be entered into Shark, which is HIVE on Spark.

Listing 12.2 Example Query to Find Top Device Types in the United States

```
SELECT device_type, sum(plays) as p FROM view1_cached WHERE country = "US"
➥GROUP BY device_type SORT BY p ORDER DESC LIMIT 20;
```

To minimize the maintenance involved in having such a large cluster, we have decided to have all ColumnFamilys use LeveledCompaction. For use cases like ours, SizeTieredCompaction can provide better performance, but it requires lots of free disk space, which has caused issues for us in the past. We're happy to take the small performance hit to get an easier-to-manage system.

When building our newest hardware cluster, we had some tough decisions to make about what disks to buy and how to present them to Cassandra. We've used Linux MDRAID extensively in RAID5 and RAID10 configurations. Both work fine with ext4 or XFS file systems. What we really wanted was the efficiency of RAID5, but with more flexibility so we can run Mesos and Spark on the same hardware. When it comes to data integrity and ease of management, ZFS is a great choice, especially when dealing with lumbering 3TB and 4TB hard drives. We tested ZFS-on-Linux on a couple of nodes in one of our production clusters and found it to be stable, so we moved forward with it. We have around 3TB of raw storage managed by ZFS today and have not had any issues with the software. When our storage starts to get busy, we can look at using one SSD per server for more caching and to store the write journal using ZFS's built-in features.

Putting all this together has allowed Ooyala to create a worldwide network for video and the analytics to help our customers power and make decisions concerning their content. Companies like Telstra, ESPN, Miramax, and Bloomberg use our Cassandra-powered system to aid in their planning, creation, and distribution of video. For more information, visit www.ooyala.com.

Hailo

Dominic Wong

Hailo is the world's biggest taxi app, connecting passengers and drivers in cities around the world. However, to call it just a taxi app would vastly underplay what the platform does. While the main passenger-facing app is fairly simple (and deliberately so), the underlying services that power the platform are much more complex. In addition to the allocation engine that matches passengers to drivers, we have systems that handle payments, traffic alerts, communications, data analysis, and more. With so many moving parts, it's vital that we have a powerful and flexible platform based on technologies that can grow and adapt as we do.

When the company started in 2011, it was just a handful of developers working as hard and as fast as they could to produce a game-changing system. The data store of choice was MySQL, which has the main benefits of being free to run and familiar to use for most developers; relational databases have been around for over 40 years and are a core part of most university computer science courses. Fast-forward to August 2013; we're in 12 cities across the globe and we've moved to using Cassandra almost exclusively. So why the shift from the familiar and warm embrace of MySQL to the relative unknown of Cassandra?

Taking the Leap

We launched in our first city, London, in November 2011 and quickly established ourselves as the number-one e-hail app in the city. We knew that we would need to expand quickly and effectively to capture key markets but stay within the financial and people constraints of a start-up. This meant that everything we did needed to be based on the principles of being distributed, resilient, and operationally simple. Sticking to these guiding principles would help us to scale effectively.

Like a lot of start-ups, we run on Amazon Web Services. The combination of AWS and Cassandra has enabled us to achieve active-active inter-data-center replication with a small team that has relatively little experience in maintaining a Cassandra installation. If we attempted the same thing with MySQL, we would have to upgrade to the paid-for clustered product and set up sharding to aid horizontal scalability. That is not impossible, but it is certainly costlier to set up and maintain in terms of money and man-hours. In contrast, Cassandra was designed from the outset to be horizontally scalable and deal with very large clusters of many terabytes. When we took into consideration the cost (free), Cassandra became a compelling proposition that we had to try.

Our typical Cassandra cluster runs across three data centers—US (east), EU (west), Asia Pacific (Tokyo)—to provide a truly global data store. In each data center, we run a node in each of three availability zones (AZ). We then set up our keyspaces with a replication factor of 3; that is, one copy in each AZ. This gives us a high level of resilience, enabling us to survive any single node or data center failure while still supporting quorum reads and writes. If we find capacity issues, we simply spin up some new machines, install Cassandra, and then add them to the ring. The entire process is fast and simple. Unlike other data storage engines, we've found that the scaling of our Cassandra clusters is a straightforward process.

We run a number of shared-use (multitenant) and single-use Cassandra clusters. The multitenant clusters are for services with relatively light demand (in terms of both volume and throughput)—any data that is updated relatively infrequently such as passenger data, payment details, and so on. Using a multitenant cluster for this sort of data means that, without negatively impacting the performance of our platform, we have fewer clusters to monitor and maintain. This is important in a start-up environment where you don't necessarily have the resources in terms of machines and people to maintain lots of different Cassandra clusters. The single-use Cassandra clusters are reserved for processes with heavy-duty usage patterns that could impact other systems if they coexisted on the same cluster, mainly statistical data with throughput of more than 1,000 writes per second. This enables us to more effectively manage our usage and target more precisely our scaling efforts. The boxes are typically m1.large instances, but our most powerful clusters are backed by SSDs for added horsepower.

Proof Is in the Pudding

So what do we actually use this scalable, distributed, resilient data store for? Like most consumer-facing companies, we need to store data about our users: names, phone numbers, e-mail addresses, and the like. We also store data about the journeys our users are making and various other facets of taking taxi rides. This all comes under the umbrella of simple entity data. For our entity data we generally use ColumnFamilys with well-known columns, mapping an entity to a row and fields to columns (see Listing 12.3). It's pretty simple stuff, and for developers who are new to Cassandra, ColumnFamilys with predefined columns and appropriate secondary indexes provide a close analog to more familiar relational DBs. This helps to soften the learning curve somewhat and enables developers who are new to Cassandra to be productive, writing services that take advantage of it fairly quickly.

Listing 12.3 **Example Customer Record from Customers ColumnFamily**

```
126007613634425612:
       createdTimestamp: 1370465412
       email: dominic@cruft.co
       givenName: Dominic
       familyName: Wong
       locale: en_GB
       phone: +447911111111
```

However, this isn't the only data we store. If it were, it would be pretty hard to justify moving from MySQL to Cassandra and all the work that migration entails. From the very beginning, we've tried to gather and record as much data about our system as we can. Every time a passenger taps to hail a taxi, every time a driver accepts payment, every time a customer registers a new card, every time something even vaguely interesting happens in our system, we record that event for future reference. It's our belief that within all of this data valuable insights can be uncovered, so we need to gather as much of that data as possible to give to our team of data geeks to reveal the hidden patterns and knowledge. This invaluable knowledge can then be fed back in to improve our service for passengers and drivers alike. This data gluttony means that we need a storage solution that can handle ever-growing volumes of data in a sustainable way.

This data is pushed from all parts of the platform to a stats service that persists the data as a time-series in Cassandra. The stats service also exposes this data as a firehose that any developer at Hailo can leverage for his or her own work. For time-series data we use ColumnFamilys with very wide rows (millions of columns), usually bucketed into days and denormalized on write for indexing (see Listing 12.4). Maintaining these indexes manually means that we need to be careful to scope and define all queries ahead of time since adding new queries post hoc requires backfill, which can be a painful process.

Listing 12.4 **Example of Time-Series Data Storing GPS Data as JSON in the Points ColumnFamily**

```
20130826:
  20130826000001-55374fa0-ce2b-11e2-8b8b-0800200c9a66: {
latitude: "51.4747404",
longitude: "-0.1758663",
timestamp: "1377475201"
  }
  20130826000002-51891bb0-ad9f-06a1-9c1d-0732206b8a21: {
latitude: "51.43520763",
longitude: "-0.16022745",
timestamp: "1377475202"
  }
```

Lessons Learned

Cassandra promises a lot—and in truth it mostly delivers on those promises—but there is no such thing as a free lunch. Any developer who is thinking about using Cassandra should be aware of its "gotchas."

Identify Your Queries Ahead of Time

While it's very easy to insert a lot of data into Cassandra, it can be somewhat harder to get that data back out. Traditional relational DBs allow ad hoc queries to be performed on tables. If you ask the question, the DB will give you the answer, although the answer may take more time if you've not defined the indexes ahead of time. In contrast, Cassandra doesn't really allow ad hoc queries; you need to be very careful to identify what queries you will need to do ahead of time and define the appropriate indexes. Unlike SQL, Cassandra doesn't allow queries on nonindexed columns, so if this is something you plan to do, you might have to think about having a separate data warehousing solution that provides such an interface.

This was a major source of frustration for our data analysts and operations teams who traditionally ran ad hoc SQL queries to gather data on the business. With a MySQL setup you can just point someone to a read-only instance and tell them to grab whatever data they need. With Cassandra this isn't really possible. Instead, we've found that the easiest thing to do is provide some mechanism to export the raw data as CSV/XML/JSON or similar format so that consumers can import it into their favorite tool.

Cassandra Doesn't Do Transactions

What this means is that with no rollback provision, in the event of failure you cannot be sure what state your data has been left in, so your systems need to take a different approach to failure recovery. Design your systems to retry failed operations and make those operations idempotent.

Idempotence is particularly important for Hailo. We use NSQ for delivering our statistics where the model for reliable delivery is based on the producer sending the same message to multiple brokers and then de-duping on the consumer side. Idempotent operations enable us to bypass the need for explicitly de-duping, which can be complicated when running a truly distributed and stateless service-oriented architecture.

Know Your Cluster

For 99% of the time, Cassandra just works and needs little to no intervention on the part of the developer. For those times that you do need to tinker or monitor, there is a great tool from DataStax called OpsCenter that graphs the performance of various aspects of your cluster to give you much greater insight into what's actually happening and could just help you identify that problem you're having.

We use a lot of open-source tools (Cassandra, ZooKeeper, NSQ, etc.). While it's tempting to just install them on the closest machine and start using them in production, you need to keep in mind that your devops team will most likely have to maintain these systems for you. So make sure they come with some great monitoring tools to keep your devops team happy.

Turn on Compression

Due to the way Cassandra stores data, turning on compression can actually give you better performance in reads and writes as well as save you storage space. The trade-off is slightly increased CPU usage, but for many this trade-off is definitely worth it.

We normally store our data as strings (JSON or just plain strings), so compression can save a lot of space in our use case. We saw around 30% space saving with compression switched on, and when you're talking about clusters with several terabytes of data, you can see the massive savings you can get.

Summary

As Hailo rolls out across the globe, we need to be sure that our platform can scale in line with our ambition. Cassandra has helped us to achieve this goal because, in our experience, it just works.

eBay

Jay Patel

eBay is one of the world's largest online marketplaces, enabling the buying and selling of practically anything. Founded in 1995, eBay connects a diverse and passionate community of individual buyers and sellers, as well as small businesses. eBay's collective impact on e-commerce is staggering; in 2012, the total value of goods sold on eBay was $75.4

billion. eBay currently serves over 120 million active users and had over 450 million items for sale as of July 2013.

eBay's Transactional Data Platform

eBay operates at an enormous scale. Every day, our data centers perform hundreds of billions of reads and writes on petabytes of data, and it's growing explosively. Simultaneously, there is an increasing demand to process data at blistering speeds. Scalability and availability are not afterthoughts at eBay; they're a primary requirement for all our systems. Our transactional data platform is a mixture of multiple SQL and NoSQL databases deployed on thousands of servers across multiple data centers. We've realized that one database really cannot solve various challenges we face at eBay and that has led us to polyglot persistence. Our transactional database platform is built on Oracle, MySQL, Cassandra, MongoDB, and XMP. We also use Hadoop/HBase for deep analytics, and our new search infrastructure, named Cassini, is built on top of it.

Why Cassandra?

There are many use cases that don't fit well in relational database systems. These include sparse data sets, data sets that require flexible schemas, or a data set that is incredibly large and requires time-series storage. Cassandra's sparse, flexible, and sorted data model has enabled us to efficiently design systems requiring storage of various kinds of semistructured data. Cassandra gives us always availability for both reads as well as writes because of its peer-to-peer (as opposed to master/slave) architecture. Its linear scalability with built-in sharding mechanisms based on consistent hashing makes data distribution painless. Anyone who has done manual sharding is aware of the pains of manually balancing the shards! Also, linear scalability on commodity hardware makes Cassandra a good fit for eBay's cloud environment where capacity requirements remain fluid.

Our databases are deployed in multiple data centers, and we always need to be ready for disaster recovery. We like Cassandra's multi-data-center support, which is baked into its architecture from the get-go. Unlike many other NoSQL databases, Cassandra gives us active-active data centers instead of active-passive. In addition to always being available, active-active data centers give us 100% local low-latency requests from the application servers to the database servers, as our application servers now never have to cross data centers. We leverage Cassandra's great write performance, distributed counters, and Hadoop to do real-time and near-real-time analytics. Cassandra's log-structured merge-tree-based internal storage enables amazing write performance. But this optimized storage engine for write workload causes compaction overhead, which can impact read performance. However, the Cassandra development team has made many optimizations to enable us to use Cassandra for multiple mixed read-write workload use cases with strict read-latency requirements. Also, Cassandra's tunable consistency enables us to have full control over the availability, partition tolerance, and consistency equation. This capability has enabled us to design many diverse use cases. Another less-talked-about benefit is that Cassandra's peer-to-peer architecture gives each node the same responsibility and roughly equal traffic load. This enables better utilization of hardware for us because we don't need to have nodes sit idle holding cold replicas or only serving read traffic. Each node in Cassandra serves reads, handles writes, and acts as replica.

Cassandra Growth

We started in late 2011 with one Cassandra cluster of eight nodes serving one use case. Now, our Cassandra deployment is more than ten clusters with more than 100 nodes spanning multiple data centers. We have over 250TB provisioned on local and shared HDDs as well as SSDs. At the time of this writing, we are getting over nine billion writes and over five billion reads in production and the volume is growing nearly exponentially.

Many Use Cases

Cassandra has enabled us to do many things that were not practical earlier. We have built a near-real-time graph-based recommendation system on top of Cassandra. This helps us compute users' taste profiles in near real time. We use Cassandra for many time-series-data-based use cases in which processing high-volume, real-time data is a top priority. These include fraud detection, order and shipment tracking, insights across many applications, pricing engine for affiliates, and mobile notification tracking, just to name a few. Another use case involves enabling social signals on eBay product pages, including like/own/want buttons and the "Your Favorites" pages on eBay.com. We have also moved our personalization system originally based on Oracle and MySQL in-memory DBs over to Cassandra. This personalization system serves real-time personalization to a user based on his or her activities on eBay.com such as browsing, buying, or selling. We also use Cassandra to store raw and aggregated metrics from thousands of production machines for monitoring and alerting purposes. Our cloud management system uses Cassandra to store cloud configuration change history. In addition, our sister companies such as RedLaser and Milo are heavy Cassandra users. They also have a large list of use cases. Since they can't all be covered here, these are two of the more interesting ones:

- Real-time insights and actions on time-series data
- Taste-Graph-based real-time recommendation system

For the other use cases, check out www.slideshare.net/jaykumarpatel/cassandra-at-ebay-cassandra-summit-2013.

Use Case: Real-Time Insights and Immediate Actions

We needed the capability to turn the enormous volumes of data that the site generates into useful insights. These insights had to be in real time, as multiple other systems needed to act in real time based on this information. The system must be able to handle terabytes of new data every day and hundreds of billions of writes. Other basic quality requirements, such as availability, scalability, and multi-data-center support, also needed to be met. This data is also of time-series nature, and we should be able to support efficient temporal queries on it. Cassandra was an obvious fit for this use case. However, we don't yet use this system for deep analytics. For deep analytics, machine learning, and offline reporting, we move data into our data warehouse environment based on Teradata, Hadoop, MicroStrategy, and many other business intelligence tools.

System Overview

As shown in Figure 12.1, raw data from the business event stream, including data on checkout, payment, shipping, and refunds, flows into multiple Cassandra clusters, where it is stored for several months or even years. From there, it feeds the fraud prevention platform, affiliate pricing engine, order tracking, real-time reporting, and other systems. We deploy multiple techniques, such as distributed counters, complex event processing, in-memory aggregations, and even combinations of these techniques, to do real-time computations. The common pattern used in all techniques is data stored in pre-aggregated form based on the target use case.

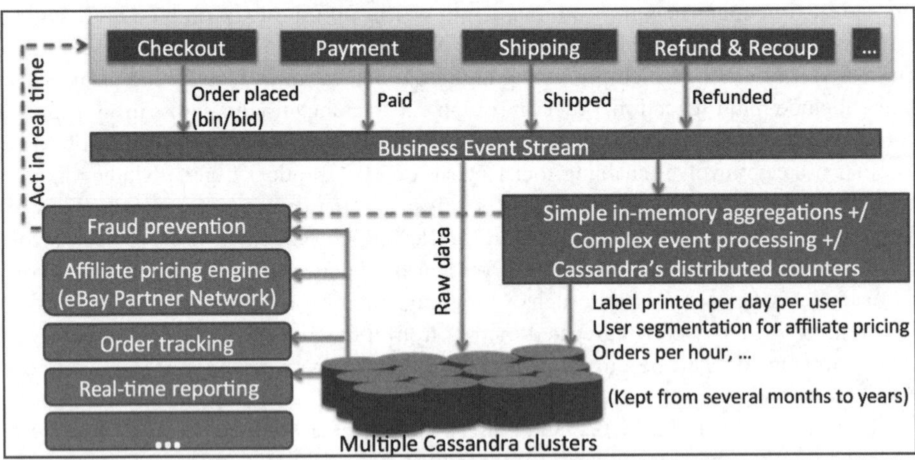

Figure 12.1 Data flow in the real-time insight platform

Data Model

Figure 12.2 is just a glimpse into the data model of many of our systems. We have dozens of ColumnFamilys depending on the use case, application requirements, and query patterns. The ones shown in Figure 12.2 are less specific and common among nearly all our use cases. As shown, the Raw Event Data ColumnFamily stores raw event data sorted by time. For this ColumnFamily, the column key (column name) is the time when the event occurred. Since column names are stored sorted in Cassandra, this enables physical sorting of time-series data on the disk as it enters the system. This physical sorting (versus lazily sorting data upon read) enables efficient range scans on time-series data. Note that the row key is a combination of time and event type. We can't use just the hour as a row key as it will likely create a hot spot, even when using a RandomPartitioner. Each kind of rollup, per minute or per hour, is stored in separate counter ColumnFamilys. In addition to these simple rollups, we also do complex filtering and aggregations by multiple dimensions, all in real time.

Use Case: Taste-Graph-Based Recommendation System

Another interesting use case is the graph-based recommendation system we developed on top of Cassandra. eBay is really a humongous graph of buyers, sellers, and items. We capture these relationships in Cassandra to compute taste profiles of every user in real time based on his or her activities (buy, sell, bid, etc.) on the site. These taste profiles are used to show personalized recommendations to users on the site, in real time.

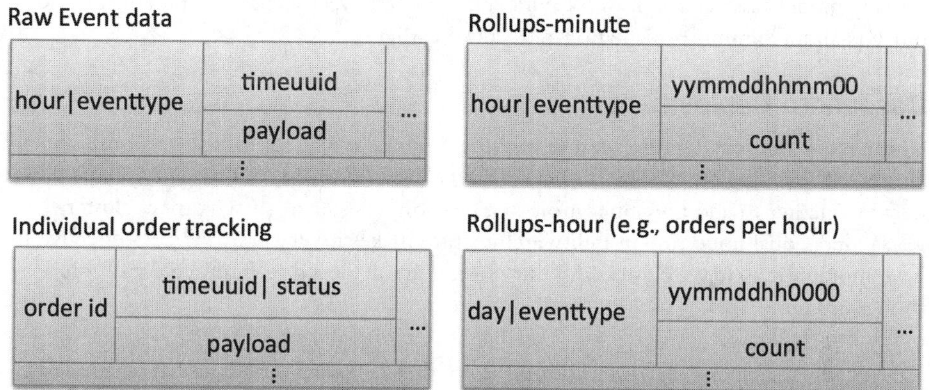

Figure 12.2 Overview of ColumnFamilys used for real-time insights

System Overview

Let's take a look at the system and data flow that power the graph.

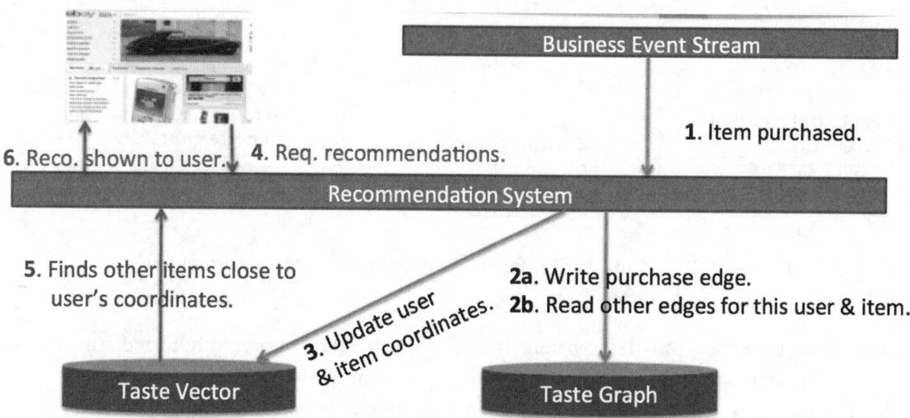

Figure 12.3 System overview of the graph-based recommendation system

As shown in Figure 12.3, whenever a user buys or bids on an item on eBay, we create a new user-item edge into the Taste Graph modeled in Cassandra. In addition to capturing this activity, we also read other edges for that user and item to compute the new Taste Vectors. That's how Taste Vectors always remain up-to-date according to users' activities on the site. Whenever that user visits any page on the site, we can show real-time recommendations based on the user's latest taste profile data. This ever-growing system handles over 600 million writes and over three billion reads per day. We're using SSDs here to support huge read demand for computing and constant updating of the Taste Vectors. However, there are some read-heavy use cases we're trying out on spinning drives to determine if we can offset costs and maintain performance. We currently have 32TB of data in the graph system, and it's growing every day. For more detail on how we actually model Taste Graph in Cassandra and how Taste Vectors are computed, check out our Cassandra Summit presentation referenced earlier.

Cassandra Deployment

Throughout our architecture, we use both dedicated clusters per use case and multitenant clusters. Depending on the use case criticality, business domain, and capacity demand, we decide whether to add the application to an existing cluster or spawn a new cluster. Cassandra's equal node responsibility architecture makes it very easy and cost-effective to have multiple Cassandra clusters. All our clusters are deployed in multiple data centers as shown in Figure 12.4.

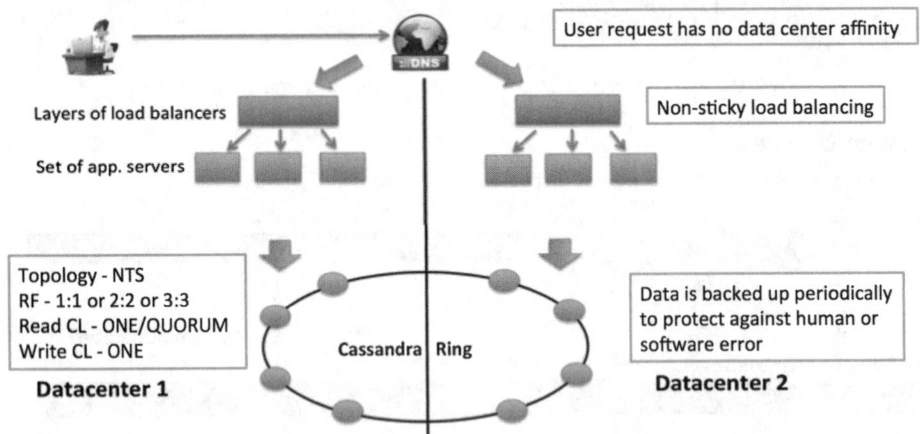

Figure 12.4 Data center layout for most of our Cassandra clusters

For some use cases, our deployment includes a third data center where we run DataStax Enterprise for its Hadoop capabilities for near-real-time deep analysis.

Currently, we're using the following hardware specifications. They are constantly evolving as our needs change and we need to adapt.

- Nodes:
- HP DL 380, 12 cores, 96GB RAM, 5.5TB RAID10 HDD

- Dell R620, 12 cores, 128GB RAM, 1TB RAID10 HDD, 10Gbps NIC
- Shared storage:
- Violin 6200/6600 flash memory array
- NetApp-based spindle storage array

Challenges Faced and Lessons Learned

One of the most difficult things we have had to deal with is the Cassandra data model. Because of the high-scale distributed nature of Cassandra, we lose the flexibility of having efficient ad hoc queries. We had to begin our designs with query patterns in mind. This method is sometimes painful and time-consuming as many of the queries may not be known up front. To support multiple query patterns efficiently, we had to duplicate data in multiple ColumnFamilys. I won't be able to discuss all the data model challenges we faced here, but for more information, you can check out our data modeling best practices slides: www.slideshare.net/jaykumarpatel/cassandra-data-modeling-best-practices.

Another challenge we've faced is to decide proper replication factor (RF) and consistency level (CL) settings for each application. Choice of RF and CL affects latency, availability, durability, consistency, and cost. Eventual consistency is great for system availability. However, designing an application for eventual consistency takes a bit of extra effort and planning. But the tunable nature of consistency is a huge plus for Cassandra as we don't need to have eventual consistency for all use cases and we can alter it on a per-use-case basis.

From the operations perspective, we have also faced many challenges in making sure Cassandra can keep up with the pending compactions given the huge amount of write traffic and data ingested. We have multiple times run into thousands of pending compactions per node. Single-threaded compaction was simply not able to keep up with the traffic and data size on each node. Reducing data size from 5TB to under 1TB per node was a big help. Also, manually splitting ColumnFamilys aided compactions in running faster for some of our use cases. Garbage collection pauses were another problem that we ran into quite frequently as a result of data size. To get around that, we did multiple optimizations, including keeping data off-heap when possible, and restricting heap size to a maximum of 8GB.

Summary

We use Cassandra very heavily at eBay. It powers applications ranging from our graph-based recommendation system to aiding in real-time insights and fraud detection. The sheer volume of data that we push through our various Cassandra clusters makes the requirement for a redundant, performant, and highly available system a daunting task. We have learned many lessons over the years, ranging from data modeling and application design to proper hardware setup and data flow. We hope that these lessons have helped you in designing and planning your Cassandra-based applications.

Appendix A

Getting Help

When you need help with Cassandra, you have quite a few options at your disposal.

Preparing Information

The first thing to do when you are looking for help is to throw together some basic information. If you are having problems with Cassandra, ensure that you have your system.log file ready along with your cassandra.yaml. These are two of the more common sources of information needed.

If you are having trouble getting code to do what you think it should be doing, be prepared with a little bit of context for what you are trying to do. In addition, have a code sample ready of what isn't working along with some sample data that you are trying to access.

IRC

Once you have put together the relevant information, head over to IRC (Internet Relay Chat). More specifically, you will find a lot of Cassandra users and developers on irc.freenode.net hanging out in #cassandra.

Mailing Lists

If IRC isn't your thing, you can always check out one of the Cassandra mailing lists. There are three primary mailing lists that might be useful.

The Cassandra-users mailing list is a general discussion list for users. This would likely be the most common place where you would go for help. The list is available at user@cassandra.apache.org.

There is also a Cassandra-developers mailing list. This is for people who are working on the Cassandra code base. The discussion typically revolves around current development progress and future plans for Cassandra. The list is available at dev@cassandra.apache.org.

The third mailing list is for driver development. The information in this list is about current and new drivers being developed for Cassandra. There is also information here about idiomatic client APIs. The list is available at client-dev@cassandra.apache.org.

Appendix B

Enterprise Cassandra

This book focuses on the open-source side of Cassandra and the freely available tools that ship with it, but there is also an enterprise ecosystem that has been built around Cassandra. Many companies offer products built on Cassandra and around Cassandra.

DataStax

DataStax offers an enterprise version of Cassandra that comes with a few additional tools. These include analytics, monitoring, and search packages with easy installation packages available for common Linux distributions. DataStax also offers full support for in-house DataStax Enterprise Cassandra installations, training sessions, and consultancy services.

The DataStax Enterprise offering comes out of the box with a few enterprise-level security features. These include internal and external authentication for database access as well as granular permissioning for better access control. Encryption options are also provided at various levels of the stack, such as file system and network traffic encryption for better security.

Apache Hadoop powers the analytics system that DataStax offers. It offers direct connectors to a number of analytics operations systems. These include Hive, Pig, Sqoop, Mahout, and MapReduce. DataStax Enterprise is not specifically a data warehouse but takes advantage of the analytics capabilities provided by Hadoop-style tools.

The search system provided by DataStax Enterprise is based on Apache Solr. This means that Cassandra can now provide full text search capability. Solr comes with the ability to give results highlighting, faceted searches (brand, type, size, etc.), rich document handling (HTML, PDF, audio and video formats, etc.), and even geospatial searches.

The major benefit that DataStax Enterprise offers is that the administrative overhead of managing complex systems like Hadoop and Solr is abstracted away from the user as much as possible. This means not having to worry about setting up all the aspects of Hadoop nodes like region servers and ZooKeeper. It also means that if you are running Solr, you don't have to think about handling sharding and redistribution of data. Cassandra handles that for you under the hood.

One of the more important aspects of the enterprise offering is OpsCenter. OpsCenter allows users not only to see what is going on in their system, but also to browse the data in Cassandra and perform normal administrative operations. Graphs can easily be created to monitor the performance of the cluster and even individual ColumnFamilys. OpsCenter also provides an alerting system for notifications of changes in your cluster. On the administration side, OpsCenter also greatly increases the ease with which backups and restores can be completed.

Acunu

Acunu is a big-data company that offers low-latency analytics as a service. Its offering of Acunu Analytics is based on Cassandra. If you remove a lot of the operational management from a big-data system, you can focus more on the core competency of your business. Acunu also offers support for Cassandra and traditional consulting.

The analytics system that Acunu has built was created to ingest high volumes of data at a high velocity. Your data is preprocessed as it enters the system. All filters, transformations, and cursory analytics are done here. This includes things like rolling up cubes of sums, averages, totals, top-K, and other common column store cubes. Pre-aggregating and grouping of queries is commonly done to ensure that when common queries are run, the responses come back quickly. The speed is achieved by storing the results of queries on the way in to ensure that queries don't need to be recalculated at query time.

Acunu also offers the option of approximate aggregates. These are things like count distinct and top-K that normally work well off of indexes in column stores but are typically very difficult or too resource intensive to do at the big-data level. If you are willing to accept an estimate of things like top-K and distinct counts in your application, this is an incredibly useful feature. An example of this feature would be something like unique visitors to a Web site or most valuable customers in a retail application. Additionally, there is the capability of supporting `GROUP BY`–style queries that can be used for hierarchical fields such as URLs or even geospatial queries.

Acunu also has a few plug-and-play capabilities. Event streams such as those from Apache Flume can easily be ingested through a RESTful API. Acunu also plugs in very well with Storm, MQ, and many common evented frameworks. Once the data has been brought into the system, you can take advantage of Acunu's AQL (Acunu Query Language), an SQL-like query language, or build JavaScript preprocessors to further filter events. This allows you to create custom groupings of data or events that more closely follow your application's needs.

Since all of the data passed into Acunu is ultimately stored in its raw form after it has been ingested and processed, additional analysis can be done on the full data set. Acunu is built on Cassandra and can therefore easily plug into Hadoop or many other common data warehouses. This gives you the ability to run ad hoc analytics or even general-purpose batch analytics.

Out of the box, Acunu also gives users the ability to create dashboards made from visualizations of the data. These visualizations come in the form of pie charts, line graphs, histograms, and other common data visualization techniques. In addition to these visualizations, there is also a visual query builder to aid in constructing complex queries. Once you have created these queries, you can turn them into reusable widgets. These can be used either on another part of the Acunu dashboard or as JavaScript, which can then be embedded into any HTML page.

Titan by Aurelius

Titan is a distributed graph database that leverages the engineering sophistication of Cassandra to encode and query graph structures efficiently at scale. Graphs are composed of vertices (dots, nodes) and edges (lines, arcs) and are leveraged when modeling domains where querying and analyzing relationships between entities or interaction between agents is important. The structure and evolution of the interactions can often provide insights that can be used to predict the future state of the system. Moreover, graphs, and the databases that persist them, provide utility as data management solutions where many-to-many relationships exist—a person having many friends, a product having many features, or a hierarchy having many branches—with cyclic, recursive data paths allowed.

Example application domains for graph databases include social networks, recommendation engines, biological systems, and financial transaction networks.

Titan stores graphs as a distributed adjacency list. Each row in Cassandra represents a vertex and its adjacency list; that is, a vertex's incident edges and properties. An edge is represented by an edge label (e.g., friendship), edge properties (e.g., rating), and a reference to the row ID of the adjacent vertex pointed to by that edge. Each edge is serialized and compressed into a column stored in the vertex's row.

Traversing, the fundamental operation on a graph, is the process of moving from vertex to vertex (i.e., row to row). To make traversing easy for developers to express, Titan relies on the open-source graph traversal language Gremlin. Determining the names of the companies that vertex 6's friends work for is expressed in Gremlin like this:

```
g.v(6).out('friend').out('worksFor').name
```

As graphs scale to the billions and trillions of edges, vertices in the graph can accumulate millions of edges. Beyond its distributed nature, one of Titan's unique advances in the graph space is vertex-centric indexes. In many ways, a vertex can be seen as a table in the relational database sense (where each row is an edge). When a table has millions of rows, an index is required to make row lookup efficient, else a linear scan of the table is required to locate rows that match the provided predicate. Titan's vertex-centric queries, leveraging Cassandra's row indexes and slice queries, allow for the efficient retrieval of a vertex's incident edges according to an edge's label or properties. For example, what companies do vertex 6's best friends work for? The following traversal "jumps" to vertex 6's friends and then to his best friends—no linear scan of all outgoing edges from vertex 6 is required.

```
g.v(6).outE('friend')
      .has('rating','best').inV
      .out('worksFor').name
```

Cassandra delivers distributed data storage technology. Titan delivers graph storage and processing technology. Together, these two technologies commingle in support of an open-source, Apache2, distributed graph database.

Pentaho

Until 2012, organizations were not able to use existing business analytics products with NoSQL databases such as Cassandra. The only way to get reports, visualizations, and analytics was via custom coding. This greatly limited the audience who could tap into Cassandra's power and made it difficult and time-consuming for those who could.

Pentaho changed that by offering the first Cassandra-based big-data analytics solution for enterprises. This integration made it possible for developers, data scientists, and business analysts to integrate and analyze both big-data and traditional data sources—and made it easy. This big-data analytics platform combines the continuous availability and extreme scalability of Cassandra with Pentaho's visual interfaces for data ingestion, manipulation, and integration, as well as data visualization, exploration, and predictive analytics.

Using Pentaho to build out a business intelligence (BI) solution with Cassandra greatly simplifies and streamlines the process. Without Pentaho, developers would spend months writing code and scripts to build simple reports and charts, and then continue to invest in maintaining that code. Only technologists with a deep understanding of Cassandra could even get to that point. Pentaho offers a visual drag-and-drop design studio, eliminating the need to code or even have a thorough understanding of the underlying technology. The ability to go beyond simple reports and charts is easy with advanced visualizations accessible via menu options. The ability to easily blend data from other sources with Cassandra data to enhance and enrich it for better analytics is also a drag and drop. What this does is drastically reduce the time and skills necessary to develop BI solutions with Cassandra.

This integrated analytics platform significantly broadened the audience beyond IT to business users and information consumers. Of equal importance was that this combined platform made Cassandra a "first-class citizen" among database technologies, no longer an isolated island with limited reach. Through Pentaho Data Integration, Cassandra is tightly woven into the broader fabric of traditional data sources and emerging new big-data techniques.

What does this all mean? This means that there are more opportunities for organizations of all sizes to tap into Cassandra's unique capabilities and get fast analytic results.

Instaclustr

Instaclustr provides managed Cassandra hosting across a wide range of cloud providers. Ranging from small development clusters to multi-data-center clusters spanning multiple cloud providers, Instaclustr allows organizations to run production-ready clusters without incurring the administration and learning overheads associated with Cassandra.

You can do things like starting a multi-data-center cluster across Amazon Web Services, Joyent, Rackspace, and others, all with a few clicks. Scaling is also managed for you with a single click/API call to increase your cluster's capacity and adjust performance. All clusters are backed up to cloud storage services, dramatically minimizing your exposure to data loss.

Given the complexity of performance tuning in Cassandra, having the ability to leverage the right configuration for your workload greatly simplifies management. Instaclustr provides a best-practices approach in an attempt to avoid the "more servers mask poor configuration" situation.

There are also enterprise-level services available through Instaclustr such as Apache Hadoop and Apache Solr. These are all available through Instaclustr-managed deployments of DataStax Enterprise. Instaclustr allows you to spend less time and resources managing Cassandra and focus on building great applications.

Index

A

O

P

Q

R

V

W

X